SRAMANA BHAGAVAN MAHAVIRA

Issued on the occasion of the 2500th nirvana anniversary

SRAMANA BHAGAVAN MAHAVIRA

LIFE & DOCTRINE

K. C. LALWANI

INDIA

MINERVA ASSOCIATES (PUBLICATIONS) PVT. LTD.
7-B, Lake Place, Calcutta-700 029
India

First Published: April 1975
ISBN: 0-88386-533-5

PRINTED IN INDIA BY DEBDAS NATH M.A., B.L., SADHANA PRFSS PRIVATE
LTD., 76 BEPIN BEHARI GANGULI STREET, CALCUTTA 700012 AND
PUBLISHED BY T. K. MUKHERJEE FOR AND ON BEHALF OF MINERVA
ASSOCIATES (PUBLICATIONS) PVT. LTD, 7-B LAKE PLACE, CALCUTTA
700 029, INDIA

TO
SUMATI CHANDJI SAMSOOKHA
IN FULFILMENT OF A PLEASANT DUTY

Man is self-surpassing
— JEAN-PAUL SARTRE

CONTENTS

CONTENTS

PREFACE

THIS UNUSUAL biography of Bhagavan Mahavira,—unusual because it views on Mahavira as a bundle of ideas rather than of facts,— was prepared under a request from the 'national committee' for the celebration of the 2500th nirvana anniversary of Bhagavan Mahavira. At its Bombay meeting sometime in June, 1974, the committee rejected this draft on the ground that it was too 'scholarly' to be of use to lay folks, and, hence. that it did not serve their purpose. The committee preferred to go ahead with a shorter and simpler work in readable Hindi by Acharya Tulsi. Later, at its Indore meeting, even this was rejected by the committee in a somewhat 'discourteous manner'. Thus credit goes to this so-called national committee for having performed two sacrifices on the auspicious occasion of the nirvana anniversary. Acharya Tulsi's work has since been resurrected by his Jaina Visva-Bharati which has issued it under its seal.

There are many biographies of Bhagavan Mahavira written in Prakrit, Sanskrit, Apabhramsa, English, and modern Indian languages, notably Hindi and Gujarati, and, therefore, the publication of one more biography in English needs justification. Except for B. C. Law's biography of Mahavira published from London in 1937, which was based on the Buddhist sources, and hence was less than a realistic picture of the man, and a recent work in Hindi in three volumes based on the discourses of Acharya Rajnis (who is an M.A. in Psychology and now calls himself a Bhagavan) who has applied the American technic of psycho-analysis to understand this man, all other biographies of Mahavira, including Gujarati and Hindi, are based on mythology and harp untiringly on the same 'facts'.

Mythology, in which all ancient accounts are recorded, because it was the language of the ancient peoples, like mathematics in modern science, is a method of magnifying a distant personality or event, and like statistics in modern times, is not much dependable for a scientific assertion. Mythology develops long after an event is past or a personality is dead, and its producer is not even in a single case an observer and eye-witness. Therefore, about any account which is based on mythology, one has to be exceptionally careful in re-presenting it to the rational minds of the present age, particularly a cross section of people outside the Jaina fold. Since biographers of Mahavira have not been sufficiently forewarned on this score, they have not exercised necessary restraint on their pen. While the present writer is prepared to go the full length with what is contained in the Anga texts, regarding subsequent works, both medieval and modern, which have invented myths of their own, he would put a heavy discount in accepting them as good accounts of the life of Bhagavan Mahavira.

Some people have preferred to conceive Mahavira in stones, and they have produced beautiful pieces of sculpture to put up Mahavira of their imagination for 'the bliss and happiness of all'. We have by now a huge collection of Jaina sculptures preserved in our museums and private collections, a fairly large number which have passed into oblivion by providing the building material for some mosque during the medieval period, a lesser number which are now worshipped as deities from the Hindu pantheon, and perhaps a still lesser number which are still lying uncared for in some wayside place waiting silently for their ultimate destruction. On the occasion of this nirvana anniversary, the preference of Bharatiya Jnanpith, Kasi, has been for Mahavira the stone, and they have planned the publication of a three volume work on Mahavira in stones, of which one volume has already come out. Interesting in itself, a piece of sculpture is the artist's conception which he engraves on stone as per the prevalent art form of his time and region. While with the passage of time mythology produces its own fruits and flowers, and may thus create a completely unrealistic image of the man, a piece of stone being barren is harmless. But this cannot be a living Mahavira, and apart from perhaps helping to some extent to fix or re-fix chronology, and adorn some museum, or satisfy the passion of a curio fan, stone serves no other purpose.

As a social scientist, the present writer is interested in Mahavira the man, a human personality, and a developed personality too, who came to find a way for himself, not as an escapist does, but as an active performer, from the artificialities and complexities of human life and to uphold it for mankind. This has been called nirvana in Jaina terminology. His exit from his father's palace is, therefore, symbolic; in so doing, he projected and lost himself beyond himself, and by dint of severe spiritual exercises over a

period of 12 years, he became the heart and centre of his own trans-
cendence, a virtual Man-God. By his precepts and practices, he
demonstrated that there was no legislator for man but man himself,
and that man, thus abandoned, must decide for, and take a leap,
himself. He demonstrated further that it was not by turning back
upon himself, but by always seeking beyond himself, an aim which
is liberation, or some loftier realisation, that man could realise
himself as truly human. In this work, Mahavira has been put up
in this new light and that provides its justification.

A critic would say that much that is contained in this volume is
not strictly due to Mahavira, but to his ganadharas and subsequent
acharyas, and that, therefore, the presentation is based on a wrong
attribution. To this, the present writer's reply would be that, in
strict sense, Mahavira gave nothing but inspiration, and what is
freely attributed to Mahavira even by the orthodoxy as his 'teachings' are also the words of ganadharas and later acharyas. The
inspiration provided by Mahavira was handed down from one
generation of monks to another, who not only preserved it in
memory, but also imparted to it a suitable expression, till at last,
after a gap of about a thousand years from Mahavira nirvana, the
whole thing was put to writing. Since then, more streams have
joined enriching the vast storehouse, and one never hesitates to
think that the whole thing is due to the master. For, as one wends
through the Agamic texts, one has the feeling that no matter whether
they were communicated by Mahavira in exactly the same form in
which they have been recorded, or were by and large the handiwork
of the acharyas, they could not have been produced by small men.

K. C. L.

Mahavira Jayanti, 1975
12 Duff Street, Calcutta 6

INVOCATION

Oh Lord ! Thy sermon profound
Sounds like a mixed note flowing from a lute,
As played by Kinnaras, the celestial musicians;
Or, like a charming music issued by gods
Wipes out all doubts at once,—
Doubts created by teacher, reason or a god.

—Jina Ballabh Suri

PART ONE

TRADITION

This sixth century B. C. was indeed one of the most remarkable in all history. Everywhere men's minds were displaying a boldness. Everywhere they were waking up out of the traditions of kingship and priests and blood-sacrifices and asking the most penetrating questions. It is as if the race had reached a stage of adolescence—after a childhood of 20,000 years.

—H. G. Wells,
A Short History of the World, p. 99

HISTORY is replete with the names of God-men, particularly the history of this country ; but here is one who made history by becoming a Man-God by dint of his own efforts.

This is Vardhamana, a Ksatriya prince, born in the Jnatri clan of the Vajjis, in the suburb of Vaisali. About the middle of his life, Vardhamana became a virtual Godhead, all-knowing and all-seeing, the master of limitless knowledge and vision. He became Mahavira, the Great Hero.

To the vast community of monks and lay followers in the Jaina order, he is Sramana Bhagavan Mahavira. To the people at large, he is simply Mahavira.

This great event took place about 600 years before the birth of Jesus Christ, about the time when 'from Athens to the Pacific the human mind was astir', when the eastern region of this country, the great land of Bharata, was passing through a religious ferment of the first magnitude, and when the traditional society here was moving out from mythology to take its place in history.

It was no accident that Vardhamana was born in India at this time. The time was propitious to receive *tirthankaras*, prophets and seers. In the Jaina view, such men come in the third and the fourth eras of each one of the up and down phases of the time-cycle to organise the order and to propound the law.

According to mythology and tradition, 23 *tirthankaras* appeared before Mahavira in the third and the fourth eras so that it had become inevitable for Vardhamana Mahavira to come and complete the train. What is, however, amazing is that before the close of the fourth era, almost a crowd of seers and prophets appeared all over the world, and the largest number in eastern India, supporting the Jaina theory that the third and the fourth eras alone are propitious for the appearance of such leaders of men, neither before when they are too advanced, nor afterwards when they are not likely to win acceptance. It was for this that the whole lot came at once.

In the sixth century B.C., people were indeed waking out of the tradition of kingship, priest-craft and blood-sacrifices ; but

5

when in a similar strain, the Indo-Aryan writers of Indian history
have presented Mahavira and Buddha as the two most successful
and illustrious leaders of reaction against Vedicism, they have
indulged in an atrocious fancy. For, neither Mahavira nor Buddha
did spearhead a reaction against anything, but produced their
own tenets which were revealed to them as an outcome of their
spiritual exertions. In other words, they knew and saw the 'truths'
themselves and propounded them. Had they really been leaders
of reaction, they would surely have been vehement against their
target, and in some form or other, this antagonism would have
found vent into the literature that is current in their names. But
nowhere in the *Agamas* or in the *Tripitakas* does one find a mention
of the Vedic religion, still less of any rancorous or malicious expression against it, which should establish that neither Jainism nor
Buddhism was a reaction, but both emerged and existed in their
own rights. Once this fact is recognised, the entire outlook of Indian
history will gain a new perspective.

Western Orientalists and their Indian counterparts created
a confusion by calling Mahavira and Buddha to be the same person.
An echo of this confusion is heard even to this day. Perhaps to
set it at rest, Orientalists like M. Guerinot (quoted by Puran Chand
Nahar in his *An Epitome of Jainism* p. 7) attempted a complete
exercise to compare the two which is as follows :

Mahavira :	*Buddha* :
1. Born at Vaisali (Kunda-gram) about 599 B.C.	1. Born at Kapilavastu about 557 B.C.
2. His parents lived to a good old age.	2. His mother died soon after giving his birth.
3. Assumed the ascetic life with the consent of his relatives.	3. Made himself a monk against the wishes of his father.
4. His preparation in the ascetic stage lasted for 12 years.	4. Obtained illumination at the end of 6 years only.
5. Died at Pawa in 527 B.C.	5. Died at Kusinagar about 488 B.C.

Another point of confusion introduced by the Orientalists

has been to call Jainism a branch of Buddhism. Thus W. S. Lolly writes:

> Buddhism in proper survives in the land of its birth in the form of Jainism. What is certain is that Jainism came into notice when Buddhism had disappeared from India.
> —Cited by C. J. Shah in *Jainism in North India*, London, 1932, Intro, p. xviii

Also H. H. Wilson has written:

> From all credible testimony, . . . it is impossible to avoid the inference that the Jainas are a sect of comparatively recent institution who came into power and patronage about the 8th and 9th century: they probably existed before that date as a division of the Bauddhas. . . .
> —*Works of Wilson*, London, 1861, Vol. I, p. 334

Thanks to the researches of two German scholars, Jainism is no longer considered to be a mere offshoot of Buddhism. Hermann Jacobi, in his Introduction to his edition of the *Kalpa Sutra*, and in his paper, "Mahavira and his Predecessors" showed that Jainism had an independent origin. George Buehler gave a scientific and comprehensive account of the birth and growth of Jainism in his article "The Indian Sect of the Jainas".

A third point of confusion has been to call Mahavira the 'founder' of Jainism, as Buddha has been called the founder of Buddhism. There is, however, a fundamental difference. For, while Buddha was himself the creator of a tradition which in course of time developed into a 'universal' religion and then disappeared from the land of its birth, Mahavira was a part of a tradition the genesis of which is lost in pre-history. The Jaina texts consider Jainism to be eternal and ever-existent, at least existent from the time when mankind conceived first the idea of religion in its most rudimentary form. Thanks to the contemporary researches in history, not only Mahavira, but his immediate predecessor, Parsva, have now been recognised as distinctly historical personages, and another, Aristanemi, the 22nd *tirthankara*, and a cousin of Lord Krisna, stands in the twilight of history. What is more, the first *tirthankara* of the Jainas has been noticed with reverence in the earliest Vedic texts, and the *Tripitakas* are full of references to a sect of monks called *niganthas* whom the followers of Buddha considered to be their most powerful adversaries. To quote Hermann Jacobi again in this connection:

> The Nirgranthas are frequently mentioned by the Buddhists even in the oldest part of the *Pitakas*. But I have not yet met with a distinct mention of the Bauddhas in any of the old Jaina Sutras, though they contain lengthy legends about Jamali, Gosala and other heterodox teachers. As it is just the reverse position to that which both sects mutually occupy in all after times, and as it is inconsistent with our assumption of a contemporaneous origin of both creeds, we are driven to the conclusion that the Nirgranthas were not a newly founded sect of Buddha's time. This seems to have been the opinion of the *Pitakas* too; for, we find no indication of the contrary in them.
>
> —*Indian Antiquary*, ix, p. 161

In a very limited sense, however, we may still call Mahavira the 'founder' of Jainism. In the Jaina view, each *tirthankara* organises his own order and gives the law. In this sense, Mahavira was a founder of Jainism, and the Jaina tradition which is extant to this day was a handiwork of Mahavira. This, however, is not to deny in any way the long tradition that existed before Mahavira.

A final point which needs be disposed of here is that in the view of observers, particularly from the God-centred religions, Jainism, which does not believe in a Creator-God, is less than a religion, and its founder may be anything but not a God-man. We have already said that Mahavira was not a God-man, but a Man-God, and his religion, the only one of its kind, stands apart from any other, traditional or modern. It is indeed the most difficult religion of the world which holds the key for man to attain the status of God. If still people find it difficult to understand Jainism, it is because

(1) they approach it with a closed mind and look for such things in the Jaina canonical texts with which they are familiar in the texts of other religions;

(2) they try to understand Jainism in terms of concepts like Deism, Pantheism, Theism, Monism, Dualism, Pluralism,

Realism, Idealism and so on and so forth, to any one of which Jainism does not even remotely fit in; and

(3) they approach Jainism as a faith, a religion in ordinary sense of the term, a routine for temple-going or visiting the monks, whereas Jainism is a way of life, and, *albeit*, the most difficult way. Basically, it is a Science for attaining Perfection, and is incidentally an Art.

In the Jaina view, the Soul, which is Reality Number One, is a conscious principle, which is in perpetual existence in space-time, and which is also in perpetual evolution towards Perfection, Enlightenment and Liberation by dint of its own *Karma*. In the process, many have been liberated in the past, and many are still under preparation for the same end in some part of the universe. Such a thing cannot be less than a religion; for, what else a religion is if not a process of self-realisation?

THE source-book on the Svetambara chapter of the tradition is the *Kalpa Sutra* by Bhadrabahu. The celebrated author delineates the life-story (*caritras*) of the *tirthankaras* of the current (*avasarpini*) phase of the time-cycle. The *Sutra* starts with a lengthy, somewhat detailed, sketch of the life of Mahavira, followed by those of Parsva and Aristanemi, the 23rd and 22nd *tirthankaras* respectively, in identical terms, though with considerable omissions to avoid repetition, and with change only in the names of personalities. Then follows a list of 20 showing the time-gap in each case from his liberation till the date of writing. The precise form is given below:

> Since the passing away of Arhat Nami (*21st*), 5,84,900 years have passed, and thereafter, of the 10th century, this is the 80th year. (*Kalpa Sutra*, 184)
> Since the passing away of Arhat Munisuvrata, 11,84,900 years have passed, and thereafter, of the 10th century, this is the 80th year. (185) And so on, . . . till
> Since the passing away of Arhat Ajita, 50 lakh-crore sagaropamas minus 42003 years 82 months passed when Mahavira was liberated. Since then nine centuries have passed, and of the 10th century, this is the 80th year. (203)

The last to receive attention of the author is Adinatha Risabha who in point of time is the first, the creator of the tradition. In other words, starting from the most recent, the author reaches one who is the farthest in time. This is perfectly sensible. If one could add the years of the time-gap, they would easily run into billions and billions and the reader is not required to stretch his imagination that far. Like our own pincode, the traditional people expressed time in fantastic figures which simply meant that the event under consideration is very very old.

The author of the *Kalpa Sutra* has not bothered about introducing lesser personalities, though nonetheless important as men-that-count (*salakapurusas*). For these, one is to turn to *Samavayanga* which provides a list of names for the following:

Kulakaras	7

Tirthankaras	24
(their fathers and mothers)	
(first female disciples)	
Cakravartis	12
(their fathers, mothers and consorts)	
Baladevas	9
(their fathers and mothers)	
Vasudevas	9
(their fathers and mothers)	
Prativasudevas	9
	total 63

Besides, the *Samavayanga* cites the names of the *tirthankaras* of the eras preceding and following our own.

A later work, belonging to the closing years of the 9th century A.D., which, again, is the source-book of the Digambara chapter of the tradition, is the *Mahapurana Trisasti-laksana-mahapurana-samgraha* by Jinasena-Gunabhadra written in Sanskrit verse. The *Mahapurana* is a huge narrative describing the lives of 63 men-that-count, as follows:

Tirthankaras	24
Cakravartis	12
Balabhadras	9
Narayanas	9
Pratinarayanas	9

Adinatha Risabha, the 1st *tirthankara*, and his son Bharata, the first *cakravarti*, have figured in the *Adipurana* part of the *Mahapurana* and the rest of the men-that-count have figured in the part called *Uttarapurana*. The entire work has 76 cantos, altogether more than 20,000 *slokas*. The entire narrative is put in the mouth of Gautama who delivered it in reply to an enquiry by King Bimbisara of Magadha. These biographies do not cover only one life of each, but 'present a detailed account of the

career of their souls through various earlier births and indicate
their march on the path of religious and spiritual progress.'

Hemacandra's *Trisasti-salaka-purusa-caritram* is a narrative
in similar lines.

In that period, at that time, people lived in the State of Nature
where life was idyllic and blissful. *The land surface being very
even, it was charming. It was like the surface of a hand-drum . . .
At that time, in Bharatavarsa, there existed from previous times
luxuriant uddalaka trees and many other flora with their roots free
from kusa and vikusa grasses. (Bhagavati Sutra, 6.7)* All the needs
of the people were taken care of by these trees. How long people
lived in this state, we cannot say; it might have been thousands
of years. Then, in the natural process, there was a change, a
metamorphosis, perhaps a natural calamity, or the sheer operation
of the law of diminishing returns, and the *uddalaka* trees became
barren. Life became increasingly difficult, and people needed a
leader who could train them up in the art of living. Such a leader
was Adinatha Risabha, son of Marudevi and Patriarch (*kulakara*)
Nabhi. With his appearance, culture enters from its 'genesis' phase
into 'creative'.

WHEN MEN WERE SIMPLE BUT IGNORANT

Within his limited capability, Nabhi tried to help his people, but
he could not achieve much. His son Risabha was one of those
men who appear at the turning point of a culture to impart to
it a sense of direction. His leadership was needed in all spheres,
social, political, economic and spiritual, and by providing it adequately and effectively, he became the Adinatha or the First Lord.

During his reign as a monarch, Risabha taught for the good
his people 72 arts, 64 woman crafts, 100 economic crafts and 3
professions. Of the 72 arts, according to the *Kalpa Sutra*, the
first in the list was writing, the most important was arithmetic
and the last one was the knowledge of the meaning of omens.
Having imparted these to his people, he anointed his 100 sons
as kings and renounced in order to be a monk.

As a monk, Risabha was the most exacting and disciplined,
and made no compromise in his life. He gave up the care of his
body, and exposed it regularly, like an unfurled flag, to austeri-

ties and hardships. Whenever a tough situation arose, he bore it in all respects, forgave it, overlooked it, believed it to be not particularly difficult a situation, nomatter whether it was created by some divine wrath, or was caused by men, animals, forces of nature or any other agency, adverse and inclement. Thus he became truly homeless (*anagara*) and tie-free (*nirgrantha*). Many who had followed in his footsteps at the time of his initiation could no longer bear the hardship and dropped out to form the lesser orders of monks like the *parivrajakas*. But Risabha went on, unperturbed by anything till he became sin-free like a conch that takes no black dot, without obstruction like the course of life, without support like the firmament, without bound like the wind, purest at heart like water in autumn, without a stain, with organs of senses withdrawn, solitary, free, ever vigilant and ever refulgent. He had no more limitation of any kind, limitation of object, place, time or subjective senses, and he became an omniscient personality, a *kevalin*, all-knowing, all-seeing, by the power of his soul, and without the aid of his organs of senses.

On his attaining omniscience, a congregation was held, widely attended, where he spoke. He organised the first order (*tirtha*) consisting of the monks, nuns, male and female followers, and became the first *tirthankara*. He named 84 *ganadharas*, and gave out *sutras, sutrarthas, dravyas, gunas, paryayas and nayas*,—all the ingredients that make a complete religion.

Risabha travelled all over the country and imparted his teachings to the people. We have it on the authority of the *Bhagavat Purana* that he visited far-off lands, 'Konka, Venkata and Southern Karnataka, in other words, the western part of the Peninsula', where people welcomed him and accepted his religion.

When at last his mission on this earth was drawing to its close, he moved to the Astapada Mountain (Mount Kaliasa) where he entered into his liberation. Risabha has been noticed with the greatest reverence in the early Vedic literature where the following hymn is dedicated to him:

> *Oh Divinity! Dost thou produce amongst us, of high descent, a god like Risabha who, by becoming an arhan, which is the epithet of the First World-teacher, may become the destroyer of enemies.*
> —*Rig-Veda* X.166

WHEN MEN WERE SIMPLE AND WISE

Compared to the early creative phase which synchronised with the life-time of one *tirthankara* only, the phase that followed which saw as many as 22 *tirthankaras* must have been very long, though, unlike the creative, this phase must have passed away without any important event. In this phase, men were simple and wise, because of which they were pious and discipline-abiding, and this made the task of the *tirthankaras* fairly easy. Even religion in this phase was less extensive than intensive (*caturyama*) and was practised as a matter of habit. As a routine, *tirthankaras* appeared from time to time, organised the order, gave out religion and named their *ganadharas*. We have the following list of them:

SERIAL	NAME	EMBLEM	CHAITYA-TREE
2nd	Ajitanatha	elephant	*saptaparna*
3rd	Sambhavanatha	horse	*salmali*
4th	Abhinandana	monkey	*sarala*
5th	Sumatinatha	goose	*priyangu*
6th	Padmaprabha	lotus	*priyangu*
7th	Suparsvanatha	*svastika*	*sirisa*
8th	Chandraprabha	moon	*naga*
9th	Subidhinatha (Puspadanta)	crocodile	*sal*
10th	Sitalanatha	*srivatsa*	*plaksha*
11th	Sreyamsanatha	rhino	*tinduka*
12th	Vasupujya	buffalo	*patala*
13th	Vimalanatha	boar	*jambu*
14th	Anantanatha	hawk	*asvattha*
15th	Dharmanatha	thunder	*dadhiparna*
16th	Santinatha	deer	*nandi*
17th	Kunthunatha	goat	*tilaka*
18th	Aranatha	*nandyavarta* (fish)	mango
19th	Mallinatha	pitcher	*asoka*
20th	Munisuvrata	tortoise	*campaka*
21st	Naminatha	blue lotus	*billva*
22nd	Neminatha	conch shell	*meghasrnga*
23rd	Parsva	snake	*asoka*

Both the Svetambara and Digambara chapters are unanimous in this that all the *tirthankaras* were Ksatriya princes, that many of them became kings before they became monks, some even rose to be *cakravartis*. The two chapters are further unanimous that none of the *tirthankaras* was faced with a challenge, as Gautama Buddha was in the form of four scenes on the streets of Kapilavastu, but renounced the world as a matter of routine, the event being preceded by a reminder from a divine agency. After being initiated into monkhood, all of them spent some time, from a few days or weeks to a few years, as monks, wandering on foot and visiting diverse parts of the country, led an austere life, and then came back to the same place (park) where initiated, to attain omniscience. At the close of their mission on earth, all except four withdrew to Sammet Sikhara (Parsvanath Hills in Bihar) where they discarded their mortal frame through a fast.

The two chapters, however, differ in certain details in some respects like the month of birth, the city of birth, names of parents, etc. Even their period of monkhood and number of *ganadharas* are not always identical. For instance, in the Digambara chapter, only two *tirthankaras* lived as monks for less than a year, in the Svetambara chapter, their number being as big as 12. There is, however, a broad similarity between the two in this that while each of the earlier *tirthankaras* named about 100 or more *ganadharas*, from the seventh *tirthankara* down, their number steadily declined, till Parsva named only 10.

Although the event finds no mention in the *Kalpa Sutra*, later writers have recorded an event in the life of Aristanemi (22nd *tirthankara*) which would look like an immediate challenge leading to his exit. Aristanemi's marriage had been finalised. As the party was proceeding to its destination, the groom saw a number of wailing animals collected in a pen. He enquired about the cause of their confinement, and was told that they had been kept by his would-be father-in-law in order to make a grand feast. This shocked Aristanemi. He released the animals with his own hands and asked his charioteer to turn the vehicle. This is the Svetambara version. In the Digambara version, the animals were detained by Krisna, Aristanemi's cousin, who was jealous of him, and who intended to rouse compassion in Aristanemi so that he would renounce the worldly life. More important are, however, the popular ballads in which the bride Rajimati has been depicted as a great heroine. She has been noticed with deep respect in the *Uttaradhyayana* and the *Dasavaikalika Sutras.*

With Parsva, we enter into history. Though there are differences about the date of his birth, it is a certainty that he was a prince from Banaras and that he propounded the religion of the four vows in which Mahavira himself was born and brought up. Later, Mahavira made modification, keeping in view the changed needs of the time.

time 3

WHEN MEN HAVE BECOME CROOKED AND CRAFTY

assisayam kiriyanam akiriyavaina hoi culassi annania
sattatthi venaiyanam ca vattisam
                    —quoted by Gunaratna in *Nandi Sutra*, 47

According to Mahavira, during his time, there were four main heretical creeds divided into 363 philosophical schools as follows:

Kriyavada	180 schools
Akriyavada	84 schools
Ajnanavada	67 schools
Vinayavada	32 schools

All these schools centred round nine 'fundamentals' of Jainism which are: *jiva* (soul), *ajiva* (non-soul), *punya* (pious deeds), *papa* (impious deeds), *asrava* (inflow of fresh *karma*), *bandha* (bondage of soul), *samvara* (stopping inflow), *nirjara* (shedding off accumulated *karma*) and *moksa* (liberation).

Kriya denotes the existence of *jiva*, etc., and those who admit the existence of *jiva*, etc., are called Kriyavadins. Various schools of Kriyavadins are centred round each one of the nine fundamentals. The point is illustrated with reference to *jiva*.

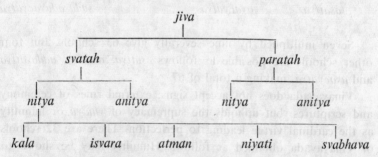

Thus we have five schools under *jiva svatah nitya*, viz., *kala*, *isvara*, *atman*, *niyati* and *svabhava*; similarly, five under *jiva svatah anitya*, five under *jiva paratah nitya* and five under *jiva paratah anitya*, in all 20 under *jiva*. By extending the same classification to each one of the fundamentals, we have nine times 20 or 180 schools of Kriyavada.

2   17

Akriyavada denies the existence of the soul, etc., for, according to this, everything is momentary, and a state comes to an end the moment it comes into existence; and when there is no continuity, there is no activity. Eighty-four schools of Akriyavada are derived from seven fundamentals (leaving aside *punya* and *papa*) as follows:

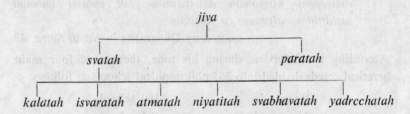

Ajnanavada denies the necessity or importance of knowledge. According to this school, knowledge is not the highest thing. Where there is knowledge, there is contradiction. *Ajnana* generates no pride, and is, therefore, in a better position to remove the bondage of the world. It had sixty-seven schools as follows: As above, let us start with *jiva*.

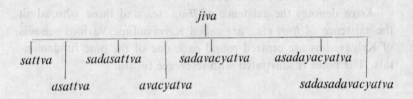

Seven multiplied by nine severally give 63 schools. But four other schools are possible as follows: *sattva, asattva, addasattva* and *avacyatva,* making a total of 67.

Vinayavada does not accept signs, external rules of ceremony and scriptures, but upholds the supremacy of *vinaya* or humility as the cardinal virtue leading to perfection. There are 32 schools of Vinayavada obtained as follows. Humility may be shown to eight classes of beings, viz., gods, master, ascetic, kinsmen, elderly people, inferiors, mother and father, and it may be shown in four ways, viz., by body, mind, speech and gifts. There are thus four-times eight or 32 schools.

The commentators Silanka, Abhayadeva and Malayagiri as well as Hemacandra accept this classification as standard.

In course of time, all these 363 schools disappeared, leaving Mahavira alone in this field. It is no wonder then that he was a *Maha Vira* or a Great Hero. We have the well-known story of Kundakaulika in which he contradicted a god who was a believer in determinism (fatalism) as propounded by Gosalaka, the founder of the Ajivaka school, and Mahavira gave his approval in the following words:

'Then you Kundakoliya answered him (the god) thus:

How, then, oh *deva*, didst thou acquire, how didst thou achieve, this thy celestial bliss, thy celestial glory, thy celestial power of a *deva*? Was it without exertion, without labour, without vigour, without manly strength?

Surely, Kundakoliya, this thy account is correct.'

For details, A. C. Sen, *Schools and Sects in Jaina Literature*, Visva-Bharati, Santiniketan, 1931.

PART TWO

LIFE

Howsoever big a pile a writer may build up in the form of essays and treatises on the life of Mahavira, the rational mind of to-day will not feel amazed at the mere size. It desires to know how much of this stands the test of Reason and how much of history.

—Pandit Sukhlal Sangavi,
Char Tirthankara, pp. 106-07

OF MAHAVIRA, as of Gautama Buddha, we have a long account of his previous births. This is so because they were not incarnations but human beings who had passed through innumerable lives before. This is not only consistent with the Indian view on rebirth but also with the Jaina theory of *karma*. Regarding Mahavira's previous births, we have record of 27 in some texts and of 33 in others. The more important of his human births are given below.

SVETAMBARA CHAPTER

The earliest on record is Mahavira's birth as Nayasara, a village overseer in West Videha. He acquired great merits by making an offer of food to hungry monks. The monks spoke inspiring words which imparted a right vision to the overseer.

1. Marici

The most important incarnation of Mahavira's soul is as Marici, son of Bharata and grandson of Risabha. Marici was greatly impressed by the honours bestowed on his grandfather after he had become a *kevalin*, and became a monk. But the rigours of a monk's life were too much for him, and he made necessary relaxations for himself, though, even now, he taught others the religion of the Jina whenever they approached him. Sometimes people would ask why he himself did not observe what he said, when Marici's usual reply was, "I am not able to bear the weight of Mount Meru."

Once, when Risabha was encamped at Vinita, Cakravartin Bharata submitted. "*Bhante !* Is there anyone in this assembly who will, like yourself, be a *tirthankara* in this land of Bharata?"

The Master pointed to Marici and said, "This son of yours will be the last *tirthankara* named Vira here in Bharata. He will be the first *vasudeva* here named Tripristha in the city of Potana, and will be a *cakravartin*, Priyamitra, in the city of Moca in the Videhas."

23

Bharata communicated it to Marici who was beside himself with joy. He jumped three steps three times and shouted, "I shall be the first *vasudeva* at Potana; in the city of Moca, I shall attain the rank of a *cakravartin*; and then I shall be the last *arhat*. Enough of anything else for me . . . My father is the first *cakravartin*; my grandfather is the first *tirthankara*. Indeed, my family is the highest."

During the life-time of Risabha, Marci never took a disciple, but directed people who came to him to the Master. After Risabha's liberation, once, when during his illness, he did not receive due attention from his brother monks, he decided to accept disciples. Marici became the founder of the *parivrajaka* sect of monks. One of his noted disciples, Kapila, became the founder of the Sankhya school of Indian philosophy.

2. Visvabhuti

At Rajagriha, there was a king named Visvanandi. By his wife Priyangu, he had a son named Visakhanandi. The king had a younger brother named Visakhabhuti who happened to be the crown-prince. Marici's soul came as a son to Dharini and Visakhabhuti. He was named Visvabhuti.

One day, when Visvabhuti was at play with his harem in the palace garden, Visakhanandi, the king's son, demanded admittance into the garden, but he was prevented by some of the guards on duty from doing so. This was noticed by some of the slave-girls from the palace who reported it to the queen. At the queen's insistence, the king gave his words to reserve the garden for Visakhanandi, but to do so, he thought of a stratagem. He ordered the military drums to be beaten, and words went round that the king would go out in order to punish a vassal chief.

When Visvabhuti came to know of this, he offered to go instead, and went out at the head of the army. But soon he realised that it was a trick. So he returned and demanded admittance into the garden. But now it was his turn to be refused. Infuriated, Visvabhuti struck an wood-apple tree with his fist, and pointing to the ground, which was covered with its fallen fruits, he said, "But for my respect for the king, I would make all their heads fall too like that."

After this incident, Visvabhuti did not stay at home. He went to Monk Sambhuti and was initiated into monkhood.

In the course of his wanderings, Monk Visvabhuti arrived at Mathura. Just then, Visakhanandi had come to the same city to marry. When his men pointed to him Visvabhuti begging, Visakhanandi became terribly angry at his sight. That very moment, Visvabhuti was knocked down by a cow, and Visakhanandi who witnessed the discomfiture had a flash of delight. Shouted he within the hearing of Visvabhuti, "Where's gone thy strength that made wood-apples drop?"

Visvabhuti heard this. He held the cow by the horn and whirled it round. Just then, he said within himself, "As a result of this austere life, may I have the strength to kill him in another birth."

3. Tripristha

At Potana, there was a king named Ripupratisatru. His wife was Bhadra. He had a son named Acala who was a *baladeva*, and a daughter named Mrigavati. Mrigavati was exceedingly charming. When she attained the full bloom of her youth, she came one day to pay her respect to her father, the king. When the king saw her, his lust was enkindled, and he set her on his lap.

The king sent for the city-elders, and when they arrived, he asked them if a jewel was produced in the kingdom, who its rightful owner would be. The elders could not anticipate what the king had in his mind, and they said thrice that the king would be its rightful owner. The king at once announced his resolve to marry Mrigavati as per the *gandharva* rites. Ashamed at such an ignoble behaviour of the king, the elders departed. Even the queen left the palace and the city, and settled in the south.

Mrigavati gave birth to a son who was named Tripristha because of his three backbones. This was none other than the soul of Visvabhuti.

At that time, there was a city named Sankhapura, of which the king was one Asvagriva, a *prati-vasudeva*. In a cave at Mount Tunga which was in the neighbourhood, Visakhanandi's soul was born as a lion. The lion ravaged the rice fields and became a source of terror to the entire city.

King Prajapati, for, Ripupratisatru was now nicknamed like this for marrying his own daughter, was a vassal king under Asva-

griva. Once the latter monarch sent a messenger named Candavega on business to Prajapati. Without caring for decorum, the
envoy rushed into the private chamber of the king who was enjoying a concert. Prajapati swallowed the affront, but not the two
princes who had the envoy beaten up.

The news of the envoy's insult reached Asvagriva at once.
He had also information about the two princes at Potana. Once
an astrologer had told him that he would be slain by one who
would insult messenger Candavega and kill the lion on Mount
Tunga. Asvagriva now demanded that Prajapati must guard the
rice fields against the turbulent lion.

As Prajapati was about to start to honour the wishes of his
superior, the two princes prevailed upon him not to go. Instead,
they offered themselves to go and guard the rice fields.

On arriving at the spot, Tripirstha enquired how and for
how long had other kings kept the lion off. He was told that 'they
came at the time of the rains (and stayed) until the gathering of
the crop'.

Tripristha was not, however, prepared to waste his time and
energy for so long a period. He preferred to weed out the root of
the trouble for good, which none so far had dared even to conceive.
Seated on the chariot, he came to the lion's den. The lion was
in, and people shouted from the sides making the lion appear with
his mouth agape.

Tripristha's ethics did not allow him to exploit the inferior
position of the lion who was without arms and without a chariot.
So he discarded his own arms and stood on the ground. The lion
noticed this, and took it as a great affront from a human being
whom he used as his food. Thought he, 'The fact that he came alone
to my cave is one piece of imprudence; dismounting from the chariot
is a second; throwing away his weapons is a third. I shall destroy
him.'

But the poor lion underrated the strength of his adversary.
As the lion jumped upon him, Tripristha seized his upper jaw
with one hand and the lower jaw with the other, and tore him
like an old linen.

At a later phase in the story, there is a duel between Tripristha,
the *vasudeva*, and Asvagriva, the *prati-vasudeva*, and the latter
fell.

4. Priyamitra

In West Videha, there was a city named Moca where reigned King Dhananjaya. His queen Dharini gave birth to a son who was named Priyamitra. To the great delight of the parents, the boy grew to be a fine youth, and then he was anointed a king.

In the course of time, Priyamitra conquered six segments of the world and became a *cakravartin*. He had a successful reign, and people were happy under his administration.

DIGAMBARA CHAPTER

The Digambara chapter has similar accounts of Mahavira's pre-births, though somewhat more detailed and slightly different. Sometimes, even names are not the same. For instance, Visvabhuti of the Svetambara chapter appears here as Visvanandi, son of King Visvabhuti of Rajagriha by his wife Jaini. Visakhabhuti, who was the king's brother, had a son named Visakhanandi by his wife Laksmana. The latter prince was an idiot. Coming to the part of the story narrating the scuffle over the garden, Visvanandi was already in, and Visakhanandi demanded admittance. The rest of the account is similar, till the prince discovered that his father had played a trick on him. He came back at once, tumbled a stone pillar in rage and went out to be a monk. Next we meet him at Mathura begging food. He was knocked down by an infuriated cow. Visakhanandi who had already lost his kingdom had come to Mathura as an envoy of some other king. He watched the incident from the top of a harlot's home in the city, and shouted in delight, "Where's gone thy strength to-day that you demonstrated once to tumble a pillar of stone?"

The rest of the account is similar again.

Coming to the account of Tripristha, in the city of Podanpur, King Prajapati had two sons, Vijaya by his queen Jayavati and Tripirstha by Mrigavati. The latter was a prodigee who was destined to be the master of half the world.

In the northern range of the Vijayardha mountain, there was a city named Vajayardhapur where reigned a *vidyadhara* named Mayuragriva. Visakhanandi's soul was born as a son unto him by Queen Nilanjana. The boy was named Asvagriva and was a little devil.

In the southern range of the Vijayardha mountain, there reigned another *vidyadhara*, King Jvalanajati, at Rathnupur. He was a powerful king, and all the rulers in the southern range were vassals unto him. He had a beautiful daughter named Svayamprabha. Jvalanajati sent an envoy to Podanpur offering his daughter's hand to Tripristha. The offer was welcomed by the other side.

Jvalanajati now started for Podanpur with his daughter. When Asvagriva heard this, he started with other *vidyadhara* kings to prevent him. Tripristha got the news and arrived in time to strengthen the army of Jvalanajati. There was a severe encounter between the two parties on Mount Rathavarta in which Asvagriva's army was completely routed. At this point, Asvagriva aimed his mighty wheel against Tripirstha. A *vasudeva* as Tripristha was, the wheel hovered round his head, and adorned his right hand. Tripristha killed his adversary with the same wheel.

The Digamvara chapter has an impressive account of Mahavira's incarnation as a lion with which we conclude. The lion lived on the top of the Himalayas east of Singhakuti. It had a dreary look and sharp teeth and claws. One day, he saw a deer, and at once took it in his mouth. Just then, two *carana* monks were flying over him. One of them saw this, and, remembering the *tirthankara*'s words, he came down with his companion. After the two were seated on a slab of stone in front of the lion, the monk spoke soul-stiring words to the lion who listened with rapt attention. The beast took the monk's counsel to his heart. He moved round and round the monks to pay them his homage. He had his memory of the previous birth revived, and he acquired the right vision to be fixed in truth. His fierceness was gone at once, and, like an actor, he stood becalmed and still. As a beast, he could court no other vow except one, and that was the most difficult vow of not taking food till death. And then

> *His body looked picture-like,*
> *His mind too was calm,*
> *Never generating fear in others,*
> 218
> *Died the lion, fixed in vow,*
> *With concentration of his mind,*
> *To be born in heaven, . . . 219*

—*Uttar-Purana*, Canto 74

IT IS a striking, though not a rare, event that a man is guided by the same star in all the important events of his life. This happened to Mahavira whose star at the time of his birth was Uttaraphalguni. It was the same asterism that was in conjunction with the moon at the time of his initiation and also at the time of his attaining the highest knowledge. Only at the time of his death, the star changed into Svati. The exact year of his birth is a matter of dispute, but we accept 599 B.C. as the year of his birth. For the rest, he was born in the first month of summer, second fortnight, thirteenth day of the bright half of the month of Caitra.

The Svetambara chapter of the tradition has the story of the transfer of Mahavira's embryo from the womb of a Brahmana woman Devananda to that of a Ksatriya queen Trisala, wife of Siddhartha, who was the chief of the Nayas (Natas), a sect in the Vajji clan. The fact of the transfer may or may not be correct, but that the tradition was pretty strong is a certainty. A piece of sculpture found at Kankalitila in Mathura depicts a god Harinegamesi in the process of transfering the embryo. This sculpture has been noticed by Vincent Smith (*The Jaina Stupa and other Antiquities of Mathura*, Plate XVIII) and by R. D. Banerjee *Lekhanukramani*, Vol. I. Plate 36), and has been identified to be as old as the second or first century B.C. The tradition was known to the author of the *Kalpa Sutra*.

A point at issue may be if such a transfer is really possible. On this, it may be said that with enormous progress in surgery, many things which were impossible in the past are possible now. Of course, this particular form of surgery, viz., transfer of the embryo from one womb to the other, is not yet a practical possibility. Accoding to the *Agamas*, though difficult, this form of surgery is possible. On an interpellation by Indrabhuti Gautama, on this particular issue, regarding the mode of transfer, Mahavira said,

> *Harinegamesi does not transfer embryo from one womb to another, nor from one womb (to be placed in another) through*

> *the uteras, nor from one womb through the uteras to be placed
> into another through the uteras; he takes out the embryo
> through the uteras and places it in the womb of another woman
> by touching the embryo with his own hands, and without
> causing any pain to the embryo. He does it with the greatest
> expertise.*   —*Bhagavati Sutra*, S. 5, U. 4

Just before conception, according to tradition, the mother of
the would-be *tirthankara* dreams 14 auspicious dreams. This had
happened to the mothers of all the *tirthankaras*, and Mahavira's
mother was no exception. Dream interpreters were called in, and
they predicted the birth of a *tirthankara* or a *cakravarti*. It appears
that interpreting dreams had been a regular profession at that
time, and there was a developed literature on this subject. After
Freud, we are now safe on this point, since none would dare say
that dream is an unreality and has no meaning.

The fourteen items in the dreams are: an elephant, an ox, a
lion, anointment, a garland, the moon, the sun, an ensign, a jar,
a lotus lake, a sea of milk, a celestial abode, a heap of jewels and
blazing flame.

As to the line in which Mahavira was born, the Buddhist texts
are silent beyond calling him 'Natapputta', 'Niganthanatha' or
'Nigantha Nataputta'. On this, Buehler writes.

> The discovery of the real name of the founder of the Jainas
> belongs to Professor Jacobi and myself. The form
> Jnatriputra occurs in the Jaina and the northern Buddhist
> Books; in Pali, it is Nataputta, and in Jain Prakrit Naya-
> putta.   —*Indian Antiquary*, VII, p. 143

This establishes beyond doubt that Mahavira was born in the
Jnatri clan of Ksatriyas. His mother Trisala was the sister of King
Cetaka of the Haihaya dynasty. Cetaka was the chief of
the Vaisali democracy, 'at whose call all the Licchavis and Mallas
rallied together for the purpose of offence and defence'. Of
Cetaka's seven daughters, six were married to six famous kings
of the time, including Nandivardhana, Mahavira's own elder
brother. This shows that the social connections of Mahavira's
father were very high.

According to Professor Rhys Davids and Cunningham, the Vajjis to which the Jnatris belonged were a large confederation which had within its fold at least eight clans (*attha-kula*) of which the Videhans, the Licchavis, the Jnatris and the Vajjis proper were the foremost. The Videhans had their capital in Mithila, but a section of them might have settled in Vaisali, and Mahavira's mother probably belonged to this section. The Jnatris had their seats at Kundapura or Kundagrama and Kollaga, both suburbs of Vaisali. The Licchavis had their capital at Vesali (Vaisali) which has been identified with Besarh (to the east of Gandak) in the Muzaffarpur district of Bihar. This city was also the seat of the entire confederation. Now, people were called 'inner Vaisalians' or 'outer Vaisalians' according as they lived in the heart of the city or they lived in the suburbia. By this criterion, Mahavira was an outer Vaisalian.

The birth of a male child in the family, not necessarily the first, is marked by celebrations all over India even to this day. It was no less so when Mahavira was born. Ever since the boy had entered into the womb, Mahavira's parents enjoyed an exceptionally good time, and therefore the happy reaction of King Siddhartha can be better imagined when he got the tidings of the birth of a male child. At once, he issued forth orders for the decoration of the city, release of prisoners, increase in weights and measures, relief of customs, etc. Then started the festivities and rituals which lasted for ten days. On the eleventh day, rites were fulfilled for the removal of impurities caused by child-birth, and on the twelfth day, a grand banquet was held where the child was named Vardhamana.

Although we do not have details about the first 30 years of his life at the palace, for the greater part of it, he lived like a prince in the midst of great opulence. This did not in any way prevent his final exit. As a boy, he was endowed with a strong and graceful body, was fearless, courageous and intelligent, and was by nature serious and grave. In other words, he had all the qualities that would forecast a great future for him. But he had no formal schooling. According to the tradition, an would-be *tirthankara* is born with a sufficient store of enlightenment to take him through life, and he needs no enlightenment from any external agency. We have a glimpse of Vardhamana as a fully grown young man in Hemacandra's monumental work wherein the savant writes,

> The Master gradually attained maturity, seven cubits tall, adorned with a beautiful gait like a forest elephant. The Lord's beauty was the greatest in the three worlds; his rank was the highest in three worlds; he had fresh manhood; yet there was no change in his nature.
>
> —translation by Helen M. Johnson, Volume VI, p. 34

Vardhamana spent 28 years of his life at the palace after which his parents died. At this point, he said to his elder brother, "Brother ! Death is always near; life is always fleeting. When this day comes, grief is no remedy. It is only the practice of *dharma* with fortitude that is fitting, but not grief which is suitable for a contemptible man."

To this, his elder brother Nandivardhana gave the following reply with his voice choked with grief: "Brother ! To-day our parents are not forgotten. To-day all their people like me are filled with grief. Will you insist on your separation at this moment?"

It is significant that Vardhamana was in no particular hurry. He spent a couple of years more at the palace, but living virtually like a monk, and preparing for the exit. At last, even Nandivardhana realised that there was no point in detaining him any further. At this point, the normal reminder came from the divine agency,

> *Awake, oh Lord, Master of the Universe,*
> *Establish Religion and Order*
> *For the well-being of all living beings.*
> *Victory be to thee, Lord, Victory be to thee !*

savvam me akaranijjam pavakammam
(All sinful acts become unworthy of my indulgence.)

WITH these words, Vardhamana initiated himself into a *chadmasta* or monk.

There was silence everywhere. Thousands of motionless eyes witnessed a superb scene on this earth.

The author of the *Kalpa Sutra* writes,

> (*He*) *was with robes on for one full year and one month. Thereafter, he became devoid of cloth, and used the hollow of his palm as his begging bowl. For slightly more than 12 years, (he) desisted from the care of the body, and at times exposed it (to hardship). During this period, when any hardship came, he bore it in all respects, forgave it, overlooked it, took it to be no hardship, howsoever severe, may be due to divine wrath, or caused by men, animals or forces of nature, or by other adverse forces.*" (*K. S.* 117)

Usually the life of a wandering mendicant is very hard, nomatter to what sect he may belong; the more so the life of a Jaina monk to whom austerity is *the* way to perfection. But austerities courted by Vardhamana as a monk were exceptional. We have the following line in the *Avasyaka Niryukti* (*Gatha* 240):

uggam ca tavokammam visesao vaddhamanassa

On this topic, once the great Sudharman said to Jambu Svami:

> Just as Svayambhu is the deepest among oceans,
> And cane-juice is the best among drinks.
> So in austerities, Vardhamana has been the foremost.

That this is no exaggeration should be clear from the fact that over a period of 12 years and 13 fortnights (4515 days) of his life as a monk, Vardhamana took food only for 350 days, and slept only once for a *muhurta* (which is equal to 48 minutes).

The *Acaranga* gives a complete account of Vardhamana's life as a monk. In his English rendering of the same, Hermann Jacobi

3   33

has captioned it as 'The Pillow of Righteousness', implying thereby that as pillow is to bed, so is hard life to righteousness.

At the time of his initiation, Vardhamana had only one cloth on his body. As he moved out on a wandering career, a Brahmana seeker approached him, and he gave to him half of it. The other half, which was on his soulder, dropped after 13 months, when he became wholly unclad.

Though he had no cover on his body, he never folded his arms to protect himself against chill, but moved with them stretched long. He never desired to protect his person, but exposed it to all weathers, to bites by insects and mosquitoes, and to touches harsh and soft.

He had virtually conquered appetite and was often on fast. Some of these were chain fasts called *pratimas* and some were long fasts with or without strings of implicit conditions. If the conditions were not fulfilled, the fast would be prolonged.

We have on record a thrilling account of one such long fast with a string of very difficult conditions attached to it. It was the twelfth year of his initiation when Vardhamana went to Kosambi. He went on a fast for an indefinite period which would break only if certain implicit conditions were fulfilled. These conditions were that he would receive boiled black lintel from the corner of a winnow from the hands of an enslaved princess, with a shaven head and iron round her feet, in tears and tired out with three days' fasting. After having taken this vow, Vardhamana moved every day in the streets of Kosambi, but as the conditions remained unfulfilled, he returned to his shelter and quietly settled into meditation. After the fast lasted for five months and 25 days, the conditions were fulfilled, and he broke his fast by receiving lintels from the hands of lucky Candana.

Vardhamana was very much restricted in his diet. Though enjoying a very good health, he took a measured quantity of food, which he begged himself without caring for what sort of reception he was accorded, though he never humbled himself before the donor. He felt no greed for dainties and delicacies, and did not at any time look for them. Whatever he got from begging, whether it was coarse food, cold food or food cooked on the previous day, whether it was lintel, barley or dry rice, he ate with peace and contentment. If, on any day, he was offered nothing, he did not feel miserable, nor did he allow this to disturb his wanderings.

Vardhamana had conquered sleep, and, as already noted, in his career as a monk, he had it only once for 48 minutes when he had 10 visions which were pertinent to his future greatness.

After his first year as a monk, Vardhamana observed silence most of the time, without caring for praise or blame.

While in meditation, he sat in various difficult postures. In winter, his preference was for a cool place, while, in summer, he exposed himself to the blazing sun.

While walking, he fixed his gaze in front of him over a stretch of ground of the size of a human being, but he never looked to the rear or to the sides. He walked with proper care, and without indulging in gossip.

For his halts, his choice usually fell on discarded cottages, inns, alms-houses, markets, smithies, kilns or gardeners' homes. Sometimes he lived in towns, and sometimes in cremation grounds, haunted homes, under a tree or a mere thatch.

He was exceptionally careless of his own body. He never took medicine, purgative, massage, etc., nor bath. He never sought to protect his person against physical tortures by village guards or security men.

At the time of his initiation, many perfumed pastes were rubbed on his body, but these were never washed afterwards, so that for four months, swarms of bees and flying insects were attracted to them. These licked the body clean, eating into his flesh and sucking his blood, but Vardhamana never lost patience with them. What to speak of killing them, he never thought or desired even to remove them from his skin.

As Vardhamana was about to start from the Jnatri-sanda park on a wandering career, a Brahmana named Soma approached him with a prayer for help. But Vardhamana had hardly anything worthwhile to give. So he shared half his garment with the beggar and placed the other half on his shoulder.

The Brahmana took the garment to a tailor to have the hem bound. The tailor advised him to get the other half, so that the two pieces together, duty repaired, would fetch them a handsome amount in the market. So the Brahmana moved out at once and followed Vardhamana like his shadow, and waiting for a chance to get it. The chance came after 13 months when Vardhamana was going from South Vacala to the North. The piece on his shoulder was caught in a thorny bush and remaind there. It was picked up by Brahmana Soma.

One incident during his first monsoon served as a turning point in Vardhamana's life. In the course of his wanderings, Vardhamana once came to a colony of the *duijjanta* monks in the outskirts of a village named Morak. The *kulapati* invied him to spend his monsoon in that colony which Vardhamana accepted. Immediately before the commencement of the rains, he arrived and occupied his cottage. The rains started, but there was an acute shortage of fooder, and cows flocked to subsist on the thatch. Thus the place lacked a peaceful atmosphere, and Vardhamana apprehended that his stay there might not be liked by other inmates of the hermitage. So he moved out at once and went to live in another village named Asthika.

At this point, Vardhamana took five resolutions which were, "(1) I shall not stay at an uncongenial place; (2) I shall meditate all the time in a statuesque posture; (3) I shall generally maintain silence; (4) I shall use the hollow on my palm as begging bowl; and (5) I shall not humble myself to any householder." These items became guidelines throughout his life.

One important event in the career of Vardhamana as a monk was his meeting with Gosalaka, who was later to become the founder of a rival sect of monks and be his leading adversary. The meeting took place at Nalanda during the second monsoon after Vardhamana's initiation when both Varadhamana and Gosalaka were sheltered in a weaver's cottage to spend the months of the rainy season there.

Gosalaka was the son of a man named Mankhali, because of which he was also called Mankhaliputra. He was named Gosalaka because he was born in a cow-shed. When the two met, Gosalaka was already a monk.

Gosalaka was impressed by the spiritual wealth of Vardhamana and requested him to accept him as his disciple. But Vardhamana remained silent. While Vardhamana was usually on fast, Gosalaka made his living by begging, but he did not leave his companion, having become his disciple from his own idea.

One month passed after this event, and then another. One

day, Gosalaka said, "I am going out to beg my food. What do you think shall I get to-day?

—"You will be given cold and impure rice, sour buttermilk and a counterfeit coin."

Gosalaka was pretty sure that he would prove him to be false. But Vardhamana's words proved correct. Ashamed at this experience, Gosalaka turned a fatalist.

Wandering from place to place with Gosalaka following, Vardhamana spent the third monsoon at Campa. In the sixth year of his wanderings, Gosalaka left him. After a gap of six months, he rejoined him, but left him again in the tenth year of Vardhamana's initiation. This time he proclaimed himself to be the leader of the Ajivakas and a *tirthankara*.

To go back to an earlier part of Gosalaka story, in the second year, Gosalaka again repeated his request to be accepted as a disciple, and this time Vardhamana agreed. In the tenth year, sometime before his exist, Gosalaka incurred the wrath of a *tapasa* monk who hurled his power-to-burn (*tejo-lesya*) at him. Vardhamana at once counteracted it by his power-to-cool (*sita-lesya*) and saved his disciple. After this incident, Gosalaka acquired the power-to-burn from him. At a later date, Gosalaka was foolish enough to burn two of Mahavira's monks with this power and to hurl it at the Master himself, but the power rebounded, and Gosalaka became a sad victim of it.

The amount of reference that we have in the Jaina *Agamas* about this man would give the impression that Mahavira had a tough time with him till he liquidated himself by his own folly.

In his career as a monk, Vardhamana visited twice the non-Aryan parts of the country, Ladha (Radha?) in the fifth year and Vairabhumi and Singhabhumi in the ninth year. He had a thought in the fifth year that upto that time, he had wandered only through the Aryan lands which were known and congenial to him; but that in order to undergo still more hardships, he must wend through alien lands. The first visit was very short. He visited the non-Aryan lands again in the ninth year, and this time he spent full six months in the pathless country, including one complete monsoon. He had terrible experiences there on both occasions. They are reproduced on the next page from the *Acaranga*.

> *In Ladha (happened) to him many dangers. Many natives attacked him. Even in the faithful part of the rough country, the dogs bit him, ran at him.* 3
>
> *Few people kept off the attacking, biting dogs. Striking the monk, they cried, 'khukkhu', and made the dogs bite him.* 4
>
> *Such were the inhabitants . . .* 5
>
> *When he who was free from desires approached the village, the inhabitants met him on the outside, and attacked him, saying, 'Get away from here.'* 9
>
> *. . . Beating him again and again, many cried.* 10
>
> *When he once (sat) without moving his body, they cut his flesh (mustaches), tore his hair under pains, and covered him with dust.* 11
>
> *Throwing him up, they let him fall, or disturbed him in his religious postures. Abandoning the care of his body the Venerable One humbled himself and bore pain, free from desire.* 12
>
> *As a hero at the head of the battle, . . . the Venerable One, undisturbed, proceeded (on the road to nirvana).* 13
>
> —Jacobi's translation, Book I, Lecture 8, Lesson 3

Although they do not toy with them, all advanced souls are inevitably in possession of supernatural or occult powers and sometimes they come out almost unwanted. Here is an instance.

In the second year, starting from Vacala, Vardhamana desired to reach Svetamvica. There were two routes, the short one which was infested with a cobra, and the circuitous which was danger-free. Vardhamana took the former despite repeated warnings from the people, who said, 'Only the wind passes; even birds do not appear.' He reached the hole and stood in meditation at its mouth. In a severe rage, the serpent rushed out, but could not burn the monk. It then gave him three bites at the feet, and was astonished to find that the man was perfectly unmoved. Said the monk,

uvasama bho candakosia
(Desist ye Candakausika)

This was enough to awaken the serpent's soul. It lived for a fortnight more repenting its misdeeds, and lying at the mouth of the hole, starving and immobile.

In his eleventh year, he was very much disturbed by a god named

Samgamaka who, in the beginning, gave him severe physical pain, and later contaminated his food. Thereon, Vardhamana gave up begging and sat in deep meditation. Ashamed, the god departed.

In the final year as a monk, he was stationed at Sumsumarapur where the Camarendra episode took place. Camara, the Indra of the Asuras, desired to dislodge Sakra, the Indra of the Devas, but was, in turn, routed by the latter, and was saved because he had taken shelter between the two legs of Monk Vardhamana. The episode has been on record in the *Bhagavati Sutra* (S. 3, U. 2.) in the form of a narrative by Mahavira himself to Indrabhuti Gautama.

In the twelfth year of his career as a monk, Vardhamana took shelter in the cottage of Brahmana Svatidatta with a view to pass the monsoon months there. The Brahmin often entered into discussions with him on complex philosophical problems and was convinced that his guest was not only a monk but also a seer. One day, said Svatidatta, 'Who is the Soul in the body?' Vardhamana replied, "He who says 'I' is the Soul."

At a much later period, in European philosophy, Descartes echoed exactly the same words: "I know that I am."

Epilogue :

In concluding this part of Vardhamana's life, we should note an important point made by Acarya Rajnis. If Mahavira was full at the time of his birth, if he had gone through all the exercises that were necessary for his own liberation, and if he was a *vitaraga* by birth, then, why did he withdraw into the life of a monk for slightly more than 12 years? According to Rajnis, he had his own 'realisation' that earned him emancipation, but to fulfil his earthly mission, he needed 'expression', for which he withdrew into monkhood. From this, we are to understand that by his own burning example, Monk Vardhamana demonstrated what right conduct was for one covetous of liberation.

IT was the thirteenth year in the life of Vardhamana as a monk when he attained the highest knowledge, *kevala jnana*, unbound by space and time, and independent of the organs of senses, including mind. This event took place on the tenth day of the bright half of the month of Vaisakha in the fourth quarter of the day on the bank of the river Rijuvaluka. A congregation was held on the spot, and as per rule, the Kevalin delivered his sermon, though he knew that 'there was no one in the assembly capable of complete self-control'.

Explaining the new position in which Vardhamana had become Mahavira, the *Agama* writes:

> Then Sramana Bhagavan Mahavira became an arhat, a jina, a kevalin, all-knowing and all-seeing. He knew and saw the grades and mutations of all the worlds including those of the gods, men, demons, etc., birth, stay and exit of all creatures in all the worlds, their migration from one life to another, from one world of existence to another, their mental thought, their deeds and enjoyments, overt or covert,—all came within the range of his unbarred vision. —*Kalpa Sutra*, 121

Because of the lack of people capable to benefit there, Mahavira, who was now devoted solely to the benefit of others, left the place at once, and having covered a distance of 12 *yojanas* during the night, he arrived at Madhyama Pava in which were assembled the wise people of the time around a great sacrifical ceremony. He settled at the Mahasena park where a second congregation met.

At the congregation, Mahavira spoke in Ardh-Magadhi, the language of the people. This tantamounted to a revolution, since it meant a dethronement of Sanskrit. The assembly was enthralled at his profound knowledge and sweetness of his voice and expression.

When the scholarly Brahmanas assembled at the sacrifice saw that instead of coming to the sacrifice ground, thousands of people were on their way to the Mahasena park, they were somewhat surprised. One Indrabhuti Gautama, a great Vedic scholar, thought that people must have been hoodwinked by some juggler. So he started with his group of 500 disciples to overpower this man.

Indrabhuti was overwhelmed at the sight of the extra-ordinary personality of Mahavira. When Mahavira saw him, he addressed him by the name and said in part as follows:

> Goyama ! You have a doubt in your mind about the existence of the soul. From the text of the Vedas, viz., that 'this massed consciousness rising from the material elements sinks back into them and perishes', you have come to the conclusion that it is from the five material elements that the conscious soul is born, and that in them it perishes; and that there is nothing like the other world. This is the source of your confusion that there is no being beyond the elements. But you are also aware that the same Vedas have a statement like 'this *atman* is of the very substance of knowledge', which clearly recognises the existence of the soul. These contradictory assertions have generated in your mind a doubt if really there is something called soul.

Continued Mahavira,

> This is not correct. The meaning of the word *vijnanaghana* in the context of the soul is that it possesses infinite knowledge infinite vision and infinite awareness. The word *bhuta* is not only matter consisting of five elements, but all objects of knowledge, animate and inanimate. Therefore, the meaning of the Vedic text is this: The soul which has infinite knowledge, infinite vision and infinite awareness acquires various categories of knowledge from various objects, and when these objects disappear or are destroyed, the categories of knowledge also disappear or are destroyed. This, however, should not create any doubt about the existence of the soul. Such is the implication of the Vedic text.

When Indrabhuti heard this synthetic interpretation and saw that Mahavira had solved his doubt which he had so far expressed to none, he was convinced that this was no ordinary human being. Indrabhuti became his first and most intimate disciple, and his first *ganadhara*.

There were ten more Vedic Brahmanas at the sacrificial ground, two of whom, Agnibhuti and Vayubhuti, were Indrabhuti's own brothers. Others were Vyakta, Sudharma, Mandita, Maurya-putra, Akampita, Acalabhrata, Metarya and Prabhasa. Each had his own disciples, but each had in his mind doubt about some fundamental item. After they heard of Indrabhuti's conversion, the whole lot followed, one after the other, to have their doubts resolved and to take shelter in the newly created order of Mahavira.

This was a big catch for the order, which had now 11 *ganadharas* plus 4400 monks, a total of 4411. In the same park, even lay follow-ers, both male and female, joined, making the order four-fold. Such a thing is called *tirtha* which is something more than a church in the Western sense. Mahavira's mission got a good start at the Mahasena park in Madhyama Pava.

Mahavira arrived at Rajagriha, the capital city of Magadha and the seat of Srenika Bimbisara. A congregation was held, atten-ded by the king and other members of the royal household. Queen Celana was already a follower of the *sramana* way. The king expressed great admiration for Mahavira. Prince Meghakumar, Nandisena and others became monks and Prince Abhaya, Sulsa and others courted the vows of lay followers. He spent the mon-soon at Rajagriha.

Mahavira's sermons at this city covered a wide variety of topics like soul, *karma*, rebirth, and the importance of human life for attaining liberation. He preached the five 'great vows', viz., non-violence, non-lie, non-sex, non-theft and non-property, and made them a must for the monks and nuns. For the lay followers, the rigidity of the five vows was somewhat reduced to make them consistent with their worldly responsibilities, but a few other items of discipline and training were supplemented.

After the rains, Mahavira reached Videha and took important disciples there. One of these, Jamali, was later to be a dissident. Having spent the monsoon at Vaisali, Mahavira reached Vatsya, and then north Kosala, and was back to Videha. The monsoon was spent at Vanijjyagrama. In the fifth year after his attainment of omniscience, he made a long trek to Sandhu Sauvira to help King Rudrayana. For the monks of the order, it was the severest ordeal to pace through the desert of Thar during the summer months.

For miles together, there was no human habitation, and prescribed sort of food and water were difficult to get.

It was the seventh year of Mahavira's career as a *tirthankara* when King Srenika of Magadha issued the following proclamation:

> If anyone be keen to join the monastic order of Bhagavan Mahavira, he should go ahead with it. His dependents will be taken care of by the state.

During the same year, an important acquisition for the *tirtha* was Ardrakakumar, a prince from Iran. So goes the story that Prince Ardraka came to Bharata, and without being instructed by anyone, he embraced the religion of Mahavira, and on reaching Rajagriha, he got himself admitted into the monastic order of Mahavira. On his way to Rajagriha, the prince defeated in discussion many persons like Mankhaliputra Gosalaka, some Buddhist *bhiksus*, Vedic scholars, some ascetics of the Sankhya school and one Hastitapasa who killed one elephant and lived on its flesh for the whole year.

In the ninth year, an important acquisition for the *tirtha* was a rich potter named Saddalaputra who was a follower of the Ajivaka religion. One night, he had a vision in which a divine voice directed him to receive a *maha-brahmana* at day break. This was no other than Mahavira himself. Henceforth, Saddalaputra became a staunch follower.

In the tenth year, a number of followers of Arhat Parsva joined the order. They held talk with Mahavira and were convinced that Mahavira was the *tirthankara* for this age. During the same year, he had important discussions with Monk Roha on sphere and non-sphere, and with Indrabhuti Gautama on the location and base of sphere. The details are contained in the *Bhagavati Sutra*.

In the eleventh year, Skandaka, a great Vedic scholar, had some of his important doubts resolved by Mahavira and joined his monastic order. Skandaka was an advanced soul, and, after joining Mahavira's order, he soon attained great spiritual heights through some of the most difficult penances under the direction of Mahavira. He was liberated on the Vipulacala. The Skandaka story is one of the most inspiring chapters of the *Bhagavati Sutra*.

In the twelfth year, one of his important disciples, Jamali, dissented from him. In the context of *karma* exhaustion, Mahavira had said that once they were set on the road to exhaustion, they were as good as exhausted. We have a corroboration of this idea in the English poet Browning who has written:

The last of life for which the first was made

But Jamali did not find sufficient proof of it in ordinary life and dissented. It is this very subtle point with which the *Bhagavati Sutra* opens. On a question by Indrabhuti Gautama, Mahavira reiterated complete support for his view expressed earlier, and Indrabhuti was fully convinced by his logic.

In the thirteenth year, Srenika Bimbisara died at Magadha, and his son Kunika succeeded him on the throne. In the following year, Kunika attacked Vaisali. The entire confederation consisting of 18 rulers came to the aid of Vaisali. But even the combined strength of so many proved insignificant, and in the great battle, King Cetaka died.

In the fifteenth year, Gosalaka clashed with Mahavira and brought about his own ignominious end. By a chance, both Mahavira and Gosalaka were camped at the same city of Sravasti. When Indrabhuti went inside the city to beg food, he heard people say that at that time there were two *tirthankaras* moving in the city. When he enquired of the Master, the latter said that Gosalaka was neither omniscient, nor a *tirthankara*. When this remark reached Gosalaka, he appeared in Mahavira's assembly to announce that he was not Gosalaka who was already dead, but that he was Kundiyayana temporarily in occupation of Gosalaka's body. When this was repudiated by Mahavira, he applied his power-to-burn. Two monks who tried to prevent him were burnt to ashes on the spot. The power was then directed to Mahavira himself. But a *tirthankara* is proof against any power, human or divine. At this point, Gosalaka declared that Mahavira would die within six months. Then Mahavira said, "Gosalaka ! I shall live for sixteen years more, but, struck by the power let loose by yourself, you will suffer from an acute fever attended with burning and die within a week. Repent you must." Gosalaka died in the same manner as Mahavira had said. His last confession was full of repentance for his past misdeeds.

Having been touched by the power released by Gosalaka, Mahavira fell ill. This was perhaps the only occasion when he was severely indisposed. He had an attack of blood dysentery from which he suffered for quite some time and had to take medicine to regain his normal health.

In the sixteenth year, there was the unification of the order of Parsva of which Monk Kesikumar was an important representative with that of Mahavira.

It was now the twenty-fourth year of Mahavira's life as a *tirthankara*. In the course of his wanderings, he came to Saketa. In the city, there lived a jewel-merchant named Jinadeva. Kirata, a non-Aryan king of Kotivarsa, was in the city as a guest of Jinadeva. He had come to buy jewels. When he saw that a large number of people were moving towards the city park, he enquired of Jinadeva where they were going. Jinadeva said that a great jewel merchant was in the city and that people were going to see him. It was at this city that Mahavira gave his discourse on *tri-ratna* or triple-jewels, viz., right knowledge, right vision and right conduct.

Thus wandering through the kingdoms of Anga, Magadha, Videha, Kosala, Kasi, Vatsa, Pancala, etc., Mahavira preached his Gospel. Many monks, heretics, scholars, men from diverse orders, sects and professions, came to him, derived inspirations from him, had their doubts resolved and questions answered, and all of them took shelter in his order.

Tirtha is more than a church. It is a complete order consisting of monks and nuns and also followers, both male and female.

A *tirthankara* is one who organises the order, and each *tirthankara* organises the order afresh. If this view be accepted, then, the present Jaina order is the handiwork of Mahavira.

Mahavira was the head of a very illustrious order. According to the *Agama*, Sramana Bhagavan Mahavira had an excellent community of 14,000 monks headed by Indrabhuti, of 36,000 nuns headed by Candana, of 1,59,000 male followers headed by Sankha-sataka, and of 3,18,000 female followers headed by Sulsa and Revati. Besides, he had in his order,—

> 300 monks who were *caturdasa-purvis* (masters of 14 *Purvas*),
> 1,300 monks who had *avadhi* knowledge,
> 700 monks who were *kevalins*,
> 700 monks who had power to transform,
> 500 monks with great intellect,
> 400 monks who were scholars,
> 700 monks who had been perfected, and
> 800 monks who were in their final body.

> *—Kalpa Sutra*, 134-145

According to another source, Mahavira's order had many
> who could curse or favour anyone by mind,
> who could curse or favour anyone by speech,
> who could curse or favour anyone by body,
> who commanded *slesmausadha-labdhi*;*
> who commanded *jallausadha-labdhi*[8]
> who commanded *viprusausadha-labdhi*; etc.

> *—Uvavaiya*, 15

This enormous growth of the order took place in 30 years. It may be recalled that at the time of his initiation, Mahavira had gone out alone, there being none following him. In the course of his wanderings, he took Gosalaka as his disciple after some

---
*Labdhi is an occult or supernatural power.

hesitation, and the latter followed him till his tenth year, after which he finally parted. Therefore, after Mahavira had attained omniscience, he started the order at his second congregation at Madhyama Pava, and in thirty years' time, at the time of Mahavira's liberation, it was a developed thing as if it had been ever existent.

There were two types of pressure on the order, one from within, and another from outside. We have already noticed that the age of Mahavira had 363 philosophical schools all centering round the Jaina fundamentals. Of all these, Gosalaka, the leader of the Ajivaka sect, caused the greatest pressure from outside. It has already been seen how this pressure got itself liquidated. Other philosophical schools proved very much less formidable and did not become at any time a major source of trouble. A new light was, indeed, emanating, from Gautama Buddha who was the junior contemporary of Mahavira, and even though the Buddhists were immensely interested in the followers of Nigantha Nataputta, and the *Tripitakas* have recorded many discomfitures about them, there was no straight clash between the two. The most significant fact is that even though Mahavira and Buddha were contemporaries for many years, and lived and moved in the same part of India, at times residing in the same city, they never met. Buddhism came up long after Gautama Buddha, say, from the time of Asoka who set it on the track to be a universal religion. But at the time of Mahavira, with the liquidation of Gosalaka, the external pressure on the order became very insignificant.

Coming to the pressure from within, at the time of Mahavira, there were many monks who belonged to the order of Parsva and who preached and practised religion based on four vows. Even Mahavira was born and brought up in the same tradition till he himself inserted five vows as the base of religion. Till these monks were finally absorbed, it appeared that the Jaina order had a twin authority, that of Mahavira and, the earlier one, that of Parsva. There are on record occasions when the monks of the order of Parsva met Mahavira, discussed their differences with him, got satisfied and joined his order.

In the *Bhagavati Sutral* (S. 5, U. 9), we have the fascinating account of the *sthavira bhagavantas*, senior monks in the order of Parsva, who met Mahavira. On a point raised by them, Mahavira said, in part, as follows:

> *Aryas* ! Arhat Parsva, the most respected of men, ordained the sphere to be eternal, without a beginning and without an end, innumerable (as space-points) and encircled (by non-sphere) ... This sphere is eternal ... The sphere exists as ever wherein there are births, deaths and transformations. It is because of these that the sphere comes to notice.

Hereafter, the monks accepted Mahavira as all-knowing and all-seeing and prayed for their inclusion in his order.

Most fascinating is, however, the account of a meeting between Monk Kesikumar of the order of Parsva and Indrabhuti Gautama, immortalised in *Addhyayana* 23 of the *Uttaradhyayana Sutra*. The venue was the Tinduka park at Hastinapur where Kesi was staying. Indrabhuti Gautama called on him. Said Kesi.

> Great Soul ! I find that Bhagavan Vardhamana lays emphasis on five vows, whereas Arhat Parsva did on four. When our goals are the same, why should there be so much difference in our ways. Why don't you feel inquisitive about it?

There followed a long discussion in the course of which a wide ground was covered. In the end, Kesi was convinced about the correctness of Mahavira's stand and said,

> *sahu goyama panna te cchinno me samsao imo*
> *namo te samsayaio savvasuttamaho yahi*

In the *Rayapaseni*, Kesi appears as a disciple of Mahavira.

Like Kesikumar, many others, notably Monk Kalasavesiyaputtra, Monk Gangeya, Pedhalaputra Udaka changed over to the religion of five vows. These accounts bring to our knowledge the history of the absorption of the remnants of the order of Arhat Parsva by the emerging order of Mahavira.

The unification of the order effected by Mahavira remained virtually in tact for several centuries after his liberation. There have been splits thereafter in organisational affairs and about details, but none of these marred the unity of the order in the fundamentals.

THE *Kalpa Sutra* is the source book on the event of Mahavira's *nirvana*. Adopted from this source, it has been elaborated in the commentaries, *curnis* and biographies. Since it was first composed, it passed through oral tradition till c. 453 A.D. when it was put to writing under the direction and leadership of Devardhi Ksamas-ramana.

Mahavira moved to Madhyama Pava to spend his last monsoon there. There must have been some sort of sentimental attachment for this place where he was spiritually born 30 years ago. He was camped at the writers' building of King Hastipala. Perfectly in good health, he was in the midst of a fast and was delivering a very long sermon, helping his followers and answering questions on times to come. In the words of the *Kalpa Sutra*:

> . . . on the exhaustion of his vedaniya karma, on the exhaustion of karma giving name, lineage and span of life, when many years of the fourth 'spoke' of the time-cycle (susama-duhsama) had rolled away, and there were only 3 years and 8½ months left for this era to close, in the very heart of Pava, at the writers' building of King Hastipalaka, all alone, and without a second person, observing a vow of taking food, devoid of water, once every third day, at a time when the moon was in conjunction with the asterism Svati, in the hour of day-break, seated in padmasana posture, reciting fifty-five chapters (of Vipaka Sutra) on the outcome of karma, and explaining the thirty-six inadequately explained chapters (from the Uttaradhyayana Sutra), as he was concentrating on the principal chapter, he passed away, went beyond the bounds of karma, was lifted up, after he had left the world, after he had cut asunder the tie of birth, old age and death, and had become perfected, enlightened and liberated, the maker of the end, the terminator of all misery. 147

In the course of his last sermon, Mahavira said, "There are four objects of existence of people in this world. Of these, wealth and love are valuable in name only; in reality, they are worthless. Liberation alone is of value and *dharma* is the road to it. The tenfold self-control, etc., is a boat for the ocean of worldly existence. Mundane life has infinite pain, but liberation has infinite bliss. There is no means for giving up the first and acquiring the second except through *dharma*. Just as a lame man may go a long way slowly, if he follows a path, so even one with the bondage of heavy *karma* may attain liberation if he practises *dharma*."

Indrabhuti Gautama bowed and said, "*Bhante* ! Arhat Risabha was at the end of the third spoke. In the fourth spoke of the present down phase, there have been twenty-three Arhats beginning with Ajita and ending with you. Please tell what will happen in future in the fifth spoke and in the sixth spoke."

Throwing light on the future, Mahavira said, "In the presence of a *tirthankara*, this land of Bharata is like a heaven full of wealth and gains, dotted with villages and towns all over. In such a period, villages are prosperous like towns, towns like heavens, common folks like kings, and kings like Kuvera (god of wealth) himself. In this period, the Acarya is like the Indra, parents are like gods, mother-in-law is like one's own mother, and father-in-law is like one's own father. In such a period, people know the distinction between the pious and the impious. They are polite, truthful, dedicated to the gods, submissive to their spiritual leaders, and firm in right conduct. Wise people are honoured in this period, conduct, learning and lineage are recognised. There are no disturbances or calamities.

When, as hereafter, *tirthankaras* will be no more, and *kevala jnana* and *manah-paryaya jnana* will disappear from the land, the state of things in Bharata will steadily deteriorate. People will have more anger and less reason; standards will be badly shaken; arrogance will wax; piety will wane making room for impiety. Villages will wear the look of creamation grounds, towns will look haunted, honest people will be subdued and crums will come up like kings. In this chaotic state, the 'logic of the fish' will be the prevailing order in which the strong will torture upon the weak. The state of things in Bharata will be like a ship without a rudder. Thieves will commit more thefts, kings will levy more taxes, and men of the judiciary will pocket more bribes. People will have a great attachment for money and grains.

The teachers' homes will lose their sanctity. They will not impart knowledge to their pupils. The students will cease to be attentive. The earth will be full of swarms of insects and bacteria. Sons will not care for their parents; daughters will be devoid of character. Charity, conduct, penance and thought,—all will sink to a low key. There will be splits and skirmishes within the spiritual orders ... *Mantras, tantras,* herbs, gems, flowers, fruits, substance, grace, life-span, fortune, bodyform, stature,— all will become very diminutive.

Conditions will be extremely miserable in the sixth spoke ... On the closing day of the spoke just preceding, conduct will disintegrate in the morning, administration at midday and fire in the afternoon. The sixth spoke will start with severe cyclones followed by torrential rains causing a complete deluge. Very few men and beasts will survive to serve as seedlings when culture again looks up, and these will somehow keep themselves alive in the holes and cravices on the banks of the Ganga and the Sindhu which themselves will dry up, and will not be wider than a chariot's route.

Striking a note of optimism in this otherwise dreary outlook, Mahavira said,

When the sixth spoke will come to an end, the first spoke of the next up phase will commence. This period will bear resemblance with the last spoke of the phase just preceding. The second spoke of the up phase will resemble the fifth spoke of the preceding down phase, and things beneficial will just begin to emerge. At the commencement of the second spoke, there will be a bracing shower which will remove heat from the earth, and more showers will follow making plant life possible again.

The environment will again become more favourable. People will come out from their holes and start living on the flat country. They will improve in physical beauty, intellect and life-span. In the third spoke, villages and towns will come up. In the fourth one, people will be born as twins, and these will live as man and wife, and their needs will be taken care of by the *kalpa* trees. And then a day will come when the up phase will come to a close. Such time cycles have appeared over an eternal past, and they will continue to appear for all times in the future. Those who will make full use of human life will break through the cycles and enter into the eternal and non-ending bliss of liberation.

This is a complete exposition on the movement of time in cycles through which cultures pass. This is not simply the Jaina view, but the Indian view which envisages time as a non-ending series of cycles consisting of the golden age, the silver age, the copper age and the iron age and the golden age again. Even peoples of other cultures have taken a similar view of time, and Arnold Toynbee has called it the 'Jewish-Zoroatsrian' view.

The final sermon lasted for 48 hours, a really superhuman job at 72 and after a fast missing six meals. But Mahavira delivered it. There were many questions and discussions. Two persons who were the last to be inducted into the order of monks by Mahavira himself were King Punyapala and King Hastipala. On a point of enquiry, Indrabhuti Gautama submitted.

> *Bhante* ! After your liberation, when will the fifth spoke commence?
> Goyama ! It will commence after the expiry of 3 years and $8\frac{1}{2}$ months.

Mahavira gave out the names of *tirthankaras, cakravartis, vasudevas, baladevas, patriarchs* and other important persons that will appear in the up phase of the time-cycle that will follow the present down phase.

Thereafter, Ganadhara Sudharma made the following submission:

> *Bhante* ! When will the sun of omniscience (*kaivalyasurya*) go out?
> Twelve years after me, Gautama will enter into liberation, and twenty years after me, you yourself will be liberated.

Sixty-four years after me, your disciple, Monk Jambu will be liberated. He will be the last omniscient of this phase. Jambu will be followed by the following in this order: Prabhava, Sayyambhava, Yasobhadra, Sambhutivijaya, Bhadrabahu and Sthulabhadra, and all of them will be the masters of 14 *Purvas*. Among these, only Sayyambhava will be the author of *Dasaveyalian* which he will write on the basis of his knowledge of the *Purvas*.

With thirty years as a householder and forty-two years in the vow, the life of Mahavira was seventy-two years. The liberation took place when 250 years had passed since the liberation of Arhat Parsva.

In their funeral oration, nine Malla chiefs from Kasi and nine Licchavi chiefs from Kosala said, "The light of spirit is out; let us lit light of matter." Light which is eternal never goes out. It rises to heaven and serves as the guiding star for all times to come.

ALTHOUGH Mahavira rose from a prince to become a Man-God, the last post of the tradition, so to say, the first post of which lies buried in pre-history, he was intensely human and remained so throughout his life. It is this basic humanism that endeared him not only to the members of his family, and, later, to his innumerable disciples and followers, but also to whosoever came in his contact. He made a lasting impression, and people felt induced to be his followers, worshippers or admirers.

We have a myth included in the *Kalpa Sutra* where the author says that when Mahavira was lodged in the mother's womb, out of consideration for his dear mother, he stopped the movement of his limbs. Perhaps his deep affection made him forget that the pain caused to the mother by the movement of the child's limbs was no pain but a pleasure to her when contrasted to the alternative situation in which she would not feel the existence of the embryo in her womb. This is what happened. When Mahavira stopped the movement of his limbs, the mother became anxious, apprehensive and nervous. Leading gynaecologists and midwives were called in and there was a complete topsy-turvy not only at the palace but all over the city. Mahavira realised this, and to relieve his mother of her anxiety, he started the movement of his limbs again.

Whatever the realistic value of this myth, the fact remains that Mahavira had great affection and regard for his parents. He never disobeyed them even at the point of inconvenience to himself, and he held no principle in life to be more sacred than the wishes of the parents. We have it in the Svetambara chapter of the tradition that Mahavira married, and even if he had taken a wife under a pressing request from the mother, that would give him more credit than discredit. As one born liberated, no one would ever believe that he ever hankered after the company of a woman, still less to parent a child; but if still he had allowed himself to be guided by the parents' wishes, this shows his great affection and admiration for them as a child. The marriage myth itself may or may not be true; but there is no denying the fact that he was intensely considerate for his parents, and this was perfectly human.

It was this affection for his parents that, in a sense, delayed his exit till his thirtieth year. For, in his mythical vein, the author of the *Kalpa Sutra* tells us, on realising the mother's agony for the child, Mahavira resolved in the womb not to renounce the world so long as his parents would be alive. This again is a child's love and consideration for his parents. For, even though the parents might know that their child was going to be a real hero by renouncing the world, no parent would relish to witness the event of renunciation. This was perfectly clear to Mahavira, and he honoured his own resolve. Immediately after the death of his parents, he sought the permission of his elder brother in order to be initiated into monkhood, but when the latter expressed distress at the idea of his separation at a time when both the parents had just passed away, he did not mind to defer further the time of his exit.

Unlike many earlier *tirthankaras* who renounced worldly life in the company of many others, Vardhamana was all alone when he went out, and till the end of his career as a monk, he was virtually alone, except for a short association with Gosalaka, about whom he never felt happy. At first, he rejected Gosalaka's request for being accepted as a disciple, but he could not persistently disoblige a companion, and so he accepted him, though Gosalaka never proved to be honest and faithful, and was always keen to prove his Master to be false. Once he separated from him, to come back again; and it was his basic love for all that induced Vardhamana to take him back. Once he had picked up trouble with some heretical monk who let loose his power-to-burn to turn Gosalaka to ashes, but Monk Vardhamana saved him. When, next, Gosalaka parted from him, and this time permanently, never to return, he became his inveterate enemy.

There was no common platform between the two. Gosalaka was a blind fatalist, while Vardhamana believed in the capacity of man. The two were poles apart. When, later, Vardhamana had become Mahavira, and Gosalaka had become the head of a rival sect, this hostility came up on the surface. But Mahavira never lost his patience with him. He retained his poise and equanimity even after Gosalaka had let loose his power to burn Mahavira, and it was on this occasion that Mahavira warned him that it was not the *tirthankara* who was to die, but Gosalaka himself on account of his innumerable sins.

After Vardhamana had become omniscient, he delivered a sermon right on the spot, but there was no one there to benefit from it. So he transferred himself to Pava covering such a long distance in one night. To quote from Hemachandra.

> Because of the lack of people worthy of benefit there, the Lord, who was devoted solely to the benefit of others, ... realising, 'I must experience much *karma*, suitable for consumption ... by the enlightenment of creatures capable of emancipation', ... went to the city Apapa adorned with noble *bhavyas*, with twelve *yojanas* of roads, inhabited by Gautama and others, worthy of enlightenment, surrounded by many disciples ...

Indeed, now he was in a hurry, and he had no time to lose. So he moved to Madhyama Pava where the country's top intellectuals were assembled at that time around a great sacrifice. This shows his enormous practical sense. That his mission was a grand success is well-known. He inducted eleven top scholars with their entire followings and these eleven were, in years to come, to be the pillars of his order.

This is a common experience in all ages. A teacher becomes great because of a great disciple. A great teacher without a great disciple is virtually lost. Krisna of the *Bhagavad Gita* had Arjuna, Jesus had St. Paul; Ramakrisna had Vivekananda. Likewise, Mahavira had Indrabhuti Gautama and other ten, but Indrabhuti was the leading-most, and, but for him, much of Mahavira would have been lost.

Another significant fact to note is that all of Mahavira's sermons were delivered, not in Sanskrit, the language of the scholars and intellectuals in ancient India, but in Prakrit, which happened to be the language of the common man, thereby giving dignity and status to the spoken dialect of the country. Later, on a query by Indrabhuti, Mahavira said that Ardha-Magadhi, the people's language, was the language of the gods. In thus deifying the common man's language, Mahavira virtually effected a revolution. This act should not be interpreted as his antagonism to Sanskrit, the language of the scholars and intellectuals, but as his love for Prakrit so that his message would go straight to everybody.

There are many biographies of Mahavira available in the market, some based on the *Agamas* and others on the Buddhist texts, but all of them, without exception, repeat the common-place, the date and place of his birth, his parents, the age at which he became a monk and then a *kevali*, his order, his liberation, some of which are already controversial items. At a distance of 2500 years, these details would appear stale. What difference does it make to a devoted heart if he was born in 599 B.C. or at any other date? And what difference does it make if his birth-place was to the north of the Ganga or to the south? This exclusive emphasis on the commonplace is the outcome of the fact that none of his erstwhile biographers is interested in Mahavira the man, and Mahavira the idea. This is a painstaking job, and hardly anyone has the time or the patience. Just as you cannot write the life-story of Ramakrisna without basing it on the *Kathamrita*, so you cannot write the life-story of Mahavira without basing it on the *Bhagavati Sutra*.

The future source-book for Mahavira's biography is, not *Kalpa Sutra*, but *Bhagavati Sutra*, wherein we get a full view of Mahavira the man and Mahavira the idea. In bulk, the *Bhagavati* is an encyclopaedia, as big as all the remaining *Agamas* taken together. But more than that, in quality, too, it is an encyclopaedia covering all branches of knowledge and one finds herein Mahavira as a true omniscient personality answering questions on diverse topics and by diverse personalities, the most dominant of whom is Indrabhuti Gautama. For some of the questions, it would appear, the answer is too obvious; but since the disciple is not impatient to repeat, so the Master is not chary to reply, each time starting with the most familiar and affectionate address, 'Goyama'. One reads the entire text as if one is hearing the dialogue straight from the Master and the disciple. Can we say the same about many other *Agamas* and on such diverse topics? And is there any other work in the entire literary history of the world which has been given with so much affection and received with so much devotion?

Mahavira organised a fourfold order consisting of the monks, nuns, male followers and female followers. In a sense, this was a routine for a *tirthankara*, and Mahavira could be no exception. In organising the order, he was fulfilling a ritual which had become a tradition. But unlike his twenty-two predecessors who lived at a time when people were simple and wise, in Mahavira's time, people became crafty and wicked so that he had to make regulations more rigorous. This he did not only for the monks but also for the lay followers, all of whom were to be lifted up to a higher spiritual elevation.

It is a characteristic feature of the Jaina *tirtha* that it is all-embracing and excludes none. In other words, the Jaina *tirtha* is inclusive, not exclusive. A monk's goal is clear. It is liberation from life's cycle of birth and death. But what about a follower? The Jaina word for a follower is *sravaka*, derived from the root *sru* which means 'to listen'. A follower is one who listens right knowledge from a right teacher in order to be fixed in right vision and to practise it in right conduct. It is no mere going to a Jaina temple or calling on a Jaina monk regularly everyday, but has a high degree of practical content. In other words, a follower's life is a preparation to monkhood, as the monk's life is preparatory to liberation. A *sravaka* who is not conscious about this responsibility is no *sravaka* in the true sense of the term. It is this that has made the Jaina *tirtha* inclusive, the first idea of *sarvodaya* or upliftment of all, as one Samantabhadra said a few centuries after Mahavira, in the human society. It is no wonder then that some of the Jaina *sravakas* even in our own time are more advanced and versatile than many men and women in the monastic order. In our own life-time, we have seen that this Jaina idea of *sarvodaya* has been used by Vinoba. If his Master, Gandhiji, got the Jaina idea of *ahimsa* and *satya* from his friend Raichandbhai and applied it in Indian struggle for freedom, the disciple, Vinoba got the idea of *sarvodaya* from the Jaina *tirtha*, and has been using it for the upliftment of the Indian society.

As the head of the order, Mahavira was a hard task-master, but without ceasing to be human. Many of his *ganadharas*, monks and lay followers were liberated during the life-time of Mahavira who had a self-imposed duty as part of his great spiritual mission to help them to attain this goal under his guidance. He was, so to say, a specialist in the science and art of liberation, and if scores of people came to him during his life-time, it was for no other purpose but to achieve this single end. We have the most inspiring story of Skandaka Parivrajaka recorded in the *Bhagavati Sutra*. This great Vedic scholar got a first-hand proof of Mahavira's spiritual eminence and placed at once the rein of his life in the hands of Mahavira. Skandaka was liberated at a time when Mahavira was alive, and the Master had had the satisfaction of seeing his devoted disciple cross through the cycle of births and deaths to reach the other bank which is immortality. Skandaka practised some of the most difficult penances, and whenever he sought permission for practising them, the Master repeated the familiar words, "Oh beloved of the gods ! Do as it may suit thy convenience, but delay not."

This Mahavira could do because death was no terror to him; on the contrary, the prudent's death was a step, and a very sure one, to immortality and eternal bliss where there was no question of separation. In our ordinary life, we love the members of our family very intensely, but when death separates us, we do not know where our dear one is gone. The space is too vast and existences are too many, and we never meet again. This is why death is a terror, a horror to us. But the people who passed through the hands of Mahavira were directed to the same destination, so that there was no probability of getting lost, and all of them were despatched to a place where they would be lodged side by side, for eternity to come, without any chance of separation. We have the following words from the lips of Mahavira spoken to his dear Goyama :

> Goyama ! *For ever, you have been attached to me with affection. For ever, you have been singing in praise of me. For ever, you are known to me. For ever, you have served me. For ever, you have followed me. For ever, you have followed my instructions. In your previous lives as a god in heaven, or as a human being on this earth, you had had a link with me, and what more, even after we die from here, when this body will be no more, we will be equals, with a common purpose, without difference.*
>
> —*Bhagavati Sutra*, S. 14, U. 7

As a hard task-master, he had his eyes everywhere. He was ever alert and mindful about his monks, disciples and followers. Once a young monk named Atimuktaka had gone out on business. He came across a rivulet, put up a sandy embankment across it, floated his begging bowl on it and shouted with joy, "My ship !

My ship." This was noticed by some senior monks of the order
who brought it to the notice of Mahavira by asking him when was
Atimuktaka going to be liberated. The Master who read through
their purpose told the monks that Atimuktaka was going to be
liberated in that very life and he admonished them strictly not to
tease, ridicule or inconvenience the young monk in any way.

With so much love for all living beings, in general, and for
his own monks and followers, in particular, Mahavira never
aloud blind affection to get over him. This explains his great emphasis on right conduct for everybody, and this also explains why
he elaborated religion to base it on five vows, instead of on four
as hitherto. He made no compromise himself, nor did he encourage
it in others. He knew it for certain that difficult times were ahead
when temptations would be many, and it would be imperative to
keep wholly apart from them. In ordinary life, we often seek short-
cuts, and we have, in fact, many; but in the progress of the spirit
to liberation, there is no short-cut. The English author Bunyan
has immortalised the difficult path of the spirit in his *Pilgrim's
Progress*. But long, long before him, Mahavira did the same for
his own followers. This is no hard-heartedness, but it emanates
from a sublime affection. In education, we often use a word,
'stretching'. A student has to be sufficiently stretched before he
becomes a scholar. In the same manner, in religion, a pilgrim has
to be sufficiently stretched before he is fit to attain his goal. In
this matter, a soft teacher is a bad teacher. If perchance the time
at one's disposal is short, the course may be intensified, but it cannot
be cut out. We have an example of this in Mahavira's own line
wherein Arya Sayyambhava produced the text of the *Dasavaikalika
Sutra* for the liberation of his dear son who had only a short span
of life on this earth. He condensed the thing, but he dropped
nothing. Such is the Jaina tradition since Mahavira, and the credit
for this goes to the great Master.

As a spiritual leader, Mahavira never lived in the ivory tower,
but was responsive to the demand of his followers, even when
such a demand meant a great personal inconvenience to himself.
During the thirty years of his life as a Head of the order, he was
constantly on his legs, and at times undertook the most arduous
treks simply because some devoted follower had desired it. In
this connection, we remember his visit to Sindhu Sauvira against

heavy odds, all to oblige the king who happened to be a devoted follower, and who had desired in his heart that the land of his country be consecrated by the touch of the Master's feet. It must be said to the great credit of the Jaina spiritual leaders to this day that they not only take long treks all on foot, even though modern travel amenities are available, they are easily accessible and amenable to discussion on any relevant thing. This is necessary for human contact. Mahavira was never chary to have contact with human beings, and in this respect the tradition he created is still a living thing in our country.

Mahavira's great love of adventure is well-known. It was, in a sense, a self-imposed discipline. We know that as a monk, he twice visited the non-Aryan lands to subject himself to the rigour of living in the midst of an alien people, and on both the occasions, he had to face the greatest hardship. But he did not care for them.

Mahavira possessed an intense sense of humour. To illustrate, once Indrabuti Gautama said,

> *Bhante ! Should we say that gods are restrained?*
> *Goyama ! Such a statement is incorrect.*
> *Bhante ! Should we say that gods are unrestrained?*
> *Goyama ! Such a statement is rude.*
> *Bhante ! Should we then call them restrained-unrestrained?*
> *Goyama ! Such a thing is very unlikely.*
> *Bhante ! Then what is to be said about gods?*
> *Goyama ! One should say that gods are non-restrained.*
> —*Bhagvati Sutra,* S. 5, U. 4

On a close perusal, it will be found that the expression 'non-restrained' is shorn of the harshness that one meets in the other expression 'unrestrained.'

If Mahavira had a genuine love for his monks and followers, the latter always held him in the highest affection and admiration. It is not surprising that while all the 23 *tirthankaras* are called *Arhat* which is an honorific title preceding their name, Mahavira alone has been called the God of the *sramanas* (*sramana bhagavan*). And of all his followers, Indrabhuti Gautama, who was the closest and the most intimate to Mahavira, had, despite his profound scholarship, a sort of blind affection for the Master on account of which he was separated by Mahavira at the time of his death. He knew for certain that Indrabhuti was incapable to take the blow, even though he knew that its duration would be short, and in overwhelming himself, he would perhaps upset the Master. Indrabhuti received the news at a distance, and as he started lamenting over this intended separation, he had the acquisition of the supreme knowledge, *kevala jnana*, and as a *kevalin*, he went beyond all joys and sorrows.

Shortly before his death, as he was busy closing his earthly account, giving out some inspiring words for his followers and initiating others into monkhood, a request had come to him from a very important quarter to the effect that he should prolong his life, if not for his own sake, at least for the sake of the larger interest of the order. The reply that he made on this occasion reveals that despite his being a Man-God, he was intensely conscious of his human status, and knew well that as a human being, he was subject to the most inexorable law of nature, viz., *man is mortal*. When it was suggested that in his absence, the order would have to face immense difficulty, he said that in the difficult times ahead, if that was to happen, he was perfectly helpless about it. The following are his memorable words;

> *kenahpi na ayuh sandhiyate kvacit*
> *duhsama bhavato badha bhavini mama sasane*

(No one, never, can increase his span of life. And if due to bad times, the order has to face difficulty, there is no redress for it.)

In his last sermon, Mahavira exhorted again on religion free from all compromises. In the words of Hemacandra, Mahavira said, in part, as follows:

> Worldly existence has infinite pain, but emancipation has infinite bliss. There is no means for the giving up of the one and acquirement of the other except through *dharma*. Just as a lame man may go a long way slowly, if he follows a path, so one even with heavy *karma* may attain emancipation, if he practises *dharma*.

Mahavira spent his last monsoon at Madhyama Pava, the place where, thirty years back, he was spiritually born, where he recruited his *ganadharas*, where he created the order. It is a normal craving of the human heart to mix up with elements at a place where he is born. Mahavira did not desire to be an exception. In this respect, a line from a song by a Bengali poet is worth quoting:

> May I die at a place
> Where I saw the light of the day.

WESTERN Orientalists identified Mahavira and his order of *nirgranthas* from the Buddhist sources and were under the wrong impression that Jainism was an offshoot of Buddhism. The impression has now been corrected.

In the Buddhist literature, Mahavira has been called Nigantha Nataputta and his followers as *niganthas*. In the entire Buddhist literature, there are, altogether, 64 references to them distributed as follows:

Pitakas	32	*references*
Majjhima Nikaya	10	,,
Digha Nikaya	4	,,
Anguttara Nikaya	7	,,
Samyutta Nikaya	7	,,
Suttanipata	2	,,
Vinaya Pitaka	2	,,

Some of these reflect on the personality of Mahavira and effort has been made to prove that it was inferior to that of Gautama Buddha. Some of these throw light on Mahavira's monks and lay followers. A reference has been made to a famine at Nalanda when, it is stated, Mahavira and his party were at Nalanda. At least three Buddhist texts refer to a split in Mahavira's camp after his death. Effort has also been made to establish that Buddha's followers were more devoted to their Master than were the followers of Mahavira.

Western Orientalists were not alone to look at Mahavira and his followers through the painted glasses of the Buddhist literature. Some Indian scholars, too, have stepped into the same fascinating trap.

This, however, is not to underrate the value of the Buddhist sources in any way. In so far as these have lent support to accounts contained in the Jaina *Agamas*, they have helped to turn the latter into historical material. Where the Buddhist sources have distorted or deviated from the truth, with our own equipment, it is not very difficult for us to visualise the reality. Though there are many areas of distortion and disagreement, the field of agreement is by no means very small.

This account of Mahavira's life, as he appeared to the Buddhists, will, therefore, be found rewarding.

Nigantha Nataputta is the name by which Mahavira was known to the Buddhists, to his own followers and even to his other contemporaries. The first title is spiritual and the second secular, describing him as a scion of the Jnatri clan. According to these texts, he was "the head of an order, of a following, the teacher of a school, well-known and of repute as a sophist, revered by the people, a man of experience, who has long been a recluse, old and well-stricken in years." According to these texts, Anga-Magadha, the territories of the Vajji-Licchavis and the Mallas and the kingdom of Kasi-Kosala were intimately associated with the wanderings of Nataputta and the activities of the *niganthas*. These texts clearly mention Vesali as the place where the religion of Nataputta found its strongest supporters among the Licchavis.

Regarding the teachings of Nigantha Nataputta, we have as follows in the *Anguttara Nikaya:*

> Whatsoever a person experiences, whether it is pleasant or painful, or neither pleasant nor painful, is due to his *karma* in the past. Hence by extenuating through penance the effect of all past deeds, and by not accumulating the effect of fresh deeds, the future gliding in rebirth is stopped; with the future gliding in rebirth stopped, the past is wiped out; with the past wiped out, ill is no more; with ill no more, painful feelings are no more; with painful feelings no more, all ill is worn out.

In the words of *Majjima Nikaya*, the steps are:

1. *kammakkhao*   (annihilation of *karma*)
2. *dukkhakkhao*   (annihilation of painful physical condition)
3. *vedanakkhao* (annihilation of painful mental condition)
4. *savvam dukkham nijjhinnam bhavissati*
   (all pains will be annihilated).

The *Anguttara Nikaya* represents Nigantha Nataputta as the exponent of the doctrine of action (*kiriyavada*). As the Jainas have accepted the world to be real, the same text jokingly writes, "The knowledge which comprehends the limited world is itself limited (*antavanta*) in its character."

The *Majjhima Nikaya* sets forth the *nigantha* argument supporting severe penances as follows:

> Beatitude cannot be reached through mundane happiness. It is attainable through the mortification of the flesh. Had it been possible to reach beatitude through mundane happiness, then, King Srenika Bimbisara of Magadha would certainly have attained it.

The early record of the Buddhists clearly attests that Nigantha Nataputta died at Pava. When the news that as soon as Nigantha Nataputta passed away, his followers started quarrelling among themselves and became divided reached Buddha, it caused him much alarm regarding the future of his own order after his death. These very records also attest that Nigantha Nataputta was alive even after Kunika had usurped his father's throne at Magadha and Devadatta had been declared by Buddha to be a wicked person.

The following references given by B. C. Law (his *Mahavira, his life and teachings*, London, 1937) to the Buddhist texts will be found interesting:

The *Culadukkhakkhanda Sutta, Majjhima Nikaya*, presents the fundamental doctrine of the *niganthas* with a criticism from the Buddhist point of view.

The *Samannaphala Sutta, Digha Nikaya*, attributes to Nigantha Nataputta certain religious discipline which was in a way the cult of the earlier *niganthas* who were the followers of Parsva.

The *Niganthuposatho, Anguttara Nikaya*, gives a description of the *uposatha* as practised by the *niganthas*.

The *Upali Sutta, Majjhima Nikaya*, hints at the fact that the lay followers of the *niganthas* were called *savakas*, not *upasakas*.

The *Samagama Sutta, Majjhima Nikaya*, names the place where Nigatha Nataputta passed away, and how, thereafter, the *niganthas* became divided into two camps.

The *Samannaphala Sutta, Digha Nikaya*, depicts Nigantha Nataputta in association with five other *tirthankaras* of that period.

Vinaya texts present some of the immediate disciples and contemporary lay followers of Nataputta. There is a *Sutta* which
paints the *niganthas* as strong advocates of vegetarian diet. There
are *Suttas* that furnish a catalogue of the punctilious ways of certain
naked ascetics of the time,—precisely those observed by the *jinakal-
pika* monks among the *niganthas*. The same set of texts introduces
the kings and the clans, and the classes of people who directly or
indirectly supported the *nigantha* movement in north India. These
very texts name the countries and places which were important
in the early history of Jainism.

Agamas and Tripitakas by Muni Nagaraj is an exhaustive study
of Mahavira and Gautama Buddha based on the texts of the two
orders. The original work in Hindi has been translated into English
by the present writer and is awaiting publication very soon.

PART THREE

PHILOSOPHY

All those who approach Jaina Philosophy will
be under the impression that it is a mass of
philosophical tenets not upheld by one central
idea, and they will wonder what could have given
currency to what appears to us an unsystematical
system ... It has, I think, a metaphysical basis
of its own which secured it a position apart
from the rival systems both of the Brahmanas
and of the Buddhists.

> —Hermann Jacobi, at the third Inter-
> national Congress for History of
> Religion, 1908

THE PROBLEM of Evil in life arises from nescience (*avidya*). Either we do not know the state of things at all, or we do not know it as it is. Hence the trouble in our life. But the Evil is not absolute. It can be eradicated by science (*vidya*).

Unlike most other religious systems of the world which have called life and the world to be unreal (*maya*), Mahavira is one of the very few spiritual leaders and world teachers who has called life and the world to be very much real. His entire philosophy, which is the same as the philosophy of the Jainas, and the religion that he propounded are based on this basic postulate.

EPISTEMOLOGY

Knowledge is the key-note of a worthy life. It is knowledge that gives a higher tone to human life. Knowledge is analysable into ideas about one's own self, about other people and about the external world; and ideas become knowledge when they are systematised and absorbed by the knower. Of course, all ideas are not derived by the same instrumentality, nor do they carry the same value or utility. Epistemology is a systematic reflection about knowledge, not only the external objects of knowledge, but also knowledge itself.

Epistemology serves a two-fold purpose. First, it supplies the key-note to the interpretation and understanding of a system of thought and culture. Second, it gives us the standpoint to have a clear and correct vision into the metaphysics of things and of thought. This is why every system of thought and culture in India begins with an exposition of epistemology. The Jainas have been one of the earliest to provide a complete epistemology.

DARSANA AND JNANA

The Jainas have two words for knowledge, *darsana* and *jnana*, for which appropriate English words may be apprehension and comprehension and if, to these, two more psychological expressions, viz., sensation and perception be added, then, we have a

complete theory of diverse phases through which knowledge is
derived.

The two words have been defined by the commentators as
follows:

> *yat samanya grahanam darsanam*
> *etad visesitam jnanam*

(Ordinary knowledge is *darsana* ; when it becomes specialised,
it is *jnana*.)

In this view, *darsana* is ordinary knowledge which is a step to
higher knowledge which is *jnana*. If we call the former to be indeterminate, then the latter becomes determinate. Strictly speaking,
they are not the obverse and reverse of the same thing, but are
distinct types. Their distinction is universally accepted by the Jaina
philosophers, and may be viewed as "a passage from the raw,
universalised stage in acquiring knowledge to a stage in which
language can be employed to clearly indicate the various elements
that have all been synthesized to form the core of knowledge, though
the emphasis on the one or the other aspects of the dichotomy
make for different expressions of the same fundamental position."
The canonical distinction between the two words should always
be kept in mind, which is that there are two distinct types of *karma*
one obstructing *darsana* and the other obstructing *jnana*, and in a
state of perfection, both must be completely annihilated.

PRAMANAS

On a query by Indrabhuti Gautama, Mahavira said, in part, as
follows:

> *There are four means of valid knowledge (pramana) which
> are perception (pratyakasa), inference (anumana), analogy
> (upamaha) and authority (agamas).*
> —*Bhagavati Sutra*, S. 5, U. 4

Pratyaksa is used to signify direct knowledge obtained by the soul
without the aid of organs of senses or of mind. It covers three
types of knowledge, viz., *avadhi, manahparyaya* and *kevala*. This
is as per *niscya naya*. As per *vyavahara naya*, knowledge derived
with the help of the organs of senses (not mind) may be called

pratyaksa. The orthodox view, however, adheres to the *niscaya naya*. When knowledge is not directly derived by the soul but comes to it through some instruments, it is *paroksa* or indirect. This covers two types of knowledge, *mati* and *sruta*.

Generally, four *pramanas* are accepted by the Jaina philosophers. But sometimes, they are reduced to three, as in the *Sthananga*, which has knocked out analogy. In later works, at times, the distinction between categories of valid knowledge and the means to derive this knowledge is just blurred over so that right knowledge becomes synonymous with *pramana*.

CLASSIFICATION OF KNOWLEDGE

The Jaina classification of knowledge as sense-perception (*mati*), testimony or authority (*sruta*), clairvoyance (*avadhi*), telepathy (*manah-paryaya*) and supreme (*kevala*) is very old, and we have authority to believe that this five-fold classification was known in the time of Parsva, and it must have come down from a still earlier period. *Mati* or *abhinivodhika* knowledge is determinate and limited and is derived by the five organs of senses, viz., eyes, ears, nose, tongue and skin, and by mind. *Sruta* knowledge is also determinate and limited and is derived by the mind and by two organs of senses, viz., eyes and ears. The source of this knowledge are the words which are the symbols of thought, gesture, etc., of some seer or seers. Since this knowledge comes from some seer or seers, it is not basically different from direct knowledge even though the knower derives it by his mind and two sense organs. According to the author of the *Nyayavatara*, "knowledge arising from words, taken in their proper acceptance, expresses reality not inconsistent with what is established by direct knowledge." *Avadhi* knowledge is also a determinate and limited knowledge of physical objects, within a limited range of space and time, derived by the knower directly, i.e., without the aid of the organs of senses and mind. *Manah-paryaya* knowledge refers to the knowledge of other's mind, also within a limited range of space and time, but again without the aid of the organs of senses and mind. *Kevala* knowledge is the unlimited knowledge of the entire reality, not limited in any way by space or time, which is derived by the soul directly, i.e., without the aid of the organs of senses and mind.

The first three forms of knowledge have three corresponding ignorances called *mati*, *sruta* and *vibhanga*. The last two forms have no corresponding ignorance, and may, therefore, be called ignorance-free.

VALIDITY OF KNOWLEDGE

Unlike some other systems of Indian philosophy, the Jaina stand about the validity of knowledge is also very clear. Valid knowledge is considered to be knowledge which illumines others as well as itself. Just as a lamp, when lit, reveals not only other objects, but also itself, so does valid knowledge. This makes all *pramanas* to be *jnana*. If *pramana* be wrong, then, an element of contradiction is introduced in which *pramana* ceases to be worth anything. In other words, a *pramana* to be the source of valid knowledge must itself be right. The standpoint is logical, sensible and correct. This is in contrast with some Indian systems wherein knowledge reveals itself alone, and with some others in which knowledge reveals, not itself, but only others, and not both simultaneously. Herein the Jaina view stands superior.

INDIRECT KNOWLEDGE

Of the five types of knowledge, the Jainas have declared the first two, viz., *mati* and *sruta*, to be indirect and mediate (*paroksa*) because here the subject, the soul, uses the instrumentality of the organs of senses and of mind to derive knowledge. In the Jaina view, the two are so extensive as to cover the following:

(i)   eight sources of knowledge of the Pauranikas, viz., inference, analogy, testimony, implication, probability, negativity, sense-perception and tradition;

(ii) six sources of knowledge of the Mimansa school (knocking out the last two items from the above list);

(iii) four sources of the Nyaya school;

(iv) three sources of the Sankhya school;

(v)   two sources of the Buddhists and the Vaisesikas; and

(vi) one source of the Carvakas.

In the quotation from the *Bhagavati Sutra* given above, we have seen that Mahavira has named *anumana*, *upamana* and *agama* as the three sources of indirect knowledge. Knowledge derived from some external mark is inference (*anumana*). Knowledge based on some similarity is analogy (*upamana*). Knowledge based on some canonical texts is testimony (*agama*). Of these three, analogy has only one type, e.g., by looking at a cow form, one may be able to say whether it is a cow, a bull or an ox. The other two need deeper consideration, but before that, we must take a more detailed view of *mati* and *sruta*.

MATI AND SRUTA

The author of the *Tattvartha Sutra* defines *mati jnana* as 'knowledge derived by the organs of senses and the mind'. In some Jaina works, two types of *mati jnana* have been mentioned, viz., one derived through the five organs of senses and the other derived with the help of the mind, while others have added a third variety which is the outcome of the joint activity of the organs of senses and the mind. The distinction is important in this that some species in the animal world which have no mind still have an experience of pleasure and pain, even great pain. For human beings, however, the instrumentality of both, viz., the organs of senses and the mind, is required to have sense perception. This is clear from the various stages in *mati* discussed by the Jaina philosophers which are cognition of sense data (*avagraha*), speculation (*iha*), perceptual judgement (*apaya* or *avaya*) and retention (*dharana*).

Avagraha develops through two stages which are contact-awareness (*vyanjanavagraha*) and object-comprehension (*arthavagraha*). In the first stage, the object in question comes into contact with a particular organ of sense by means of a transformation of its substance into the sense data perceivable by the said organ. This is a very important stage without which the second stage of object-comprehension becomes impossible and irrelevant. Contact-awareness is, however, considered possible only with regard to four organs, eyes being excepted. (Eyes have been called by the Jainas to be a non-touching organ.) *Arthavagraha* is considered to be of six varieties resulting from the activity of the five organs of senses and the mind.

Iha refers to the speculation stage that follows sensation wherein there is an attempt to know more about the object that caused the sensation. Here, the mind becomes active and wants to know precisely, and passes from a general consciousness to specific. In the words of the *Nandi Sutra* (35)

> *In sensation, a person hears a sound, but does not know whose sound it is, whereas in speculation he cognises the nature of the sound.*

Iha is to be distinguished from *samsaya* which means doubt. *Iha* represents the mind's successful attempt, through cogent reasoning and methodical analysis, to distinguish clearly between what is true and what is false.

Apaya is the stage of affirming one out of several alternatives,—'cognition of the true nature on account of the cognition of the particular characteristics'. Some commentators have viewed this to be the stage of elimination of what is unnecessary, to distinguish it from the positive affirmation of the existent qualities which is the fourth stage; but their critics are of the view that the very process which denies certain qualities affirms certain others, and that the two processes are simultaneous rather than being one after the other. The latter view which attributes positive function to *apaya* seems to be more logically consistent with the general theory of knowledge of the Jainas.

Dharana is the fourth stage which completes perceptual knowledge. This is the outcome of the transformation of the third stage wherein a perceptual judgement is arrived at. *Dharana* stands for the retention of this judgement. In this connection, the author of the *Tattvartha Sutra Bhasya* has distinguished three stages in the development of *dharana* which are, the stage where there is a positive determination of the qualities of the object of comprehension, the stage for the retention of the comprehension, and the stage where there is the ability to recognise the same on future occasions. Likewise, the author of the *Visesavasyaka Bhasya* recognises three aspects of *dharana* as absence of lapse (*avicyuti*), emergence of mental trace (*vasana*) and recollection in future (*anusmarana*).

Knowledge contained in the scriptures or knowledge of the scriptures is called *sruta jnana*. It is of two kinds, viz., that which is incorporated in the 12 *Angas* (this on the assumption of 12 *Angas*) and that which is outside the *Angas*. There are 12 varieties of the first kind and more than 12 of the second, may be as many as there are alphabets and their possible combinations. *Nandi Sutra* mentions fourteen characteristics of *sruta* of which the more important are concerned with the shape, sound, etc., of the letter (*aksara-sruta*), cognitival activities (*samjni-sruta*), right scriptures (*samyak-sruta*) and the type of mind involved (*asamjni-sruta*). According to *Avasyak Niryukti*, these fourteen characteristics are alphabet (*aksara*), cognitive (*samjnin*), right (*samyak*), having a beginning (*sadika*), having an end (*saparyavasita*), containing repetitions (*gamika*) and included in the original scriptures (*anga-pravista*), making seven, and their opposites, making 14.

Acarya Kunda Kunda has divided *sruta* into four classes as integration (*labdhi*), consideration (*bhavana*), understanding (*upa-yoga*) and interpretation (*naya*). Integration stands for the stage of explanation which needs reference to a phenomenon with which the phenomenon under consideration is related or associated. Consideration takes note of the nature of the familiar phenomenon to understand the new one. Understanding relates to the new phenomenon which is perceived. *Naya* stands for interpretation, which may be the knowledge of a thing or reality in one or the other of its particular aspects, or which may be the knowledge of a thing or reality in the totality of its aspects. The former called *nayavada* is taken care of in *naya srutas* and the latter called *syadvada* in *syadvada srutas*. The two demand separate attention and are the themes for the next chapter.

It may be worthwhile not to consider the four classes of *sruta* named by Acarya Kunda Kunda as distinctly separate but as steps to the same end which is the progressive explanation of phenomenon. As Hari Satya Bhattacharya has written,

> It is far more reasonable to look upon these processes as four steps to the progressive explanation of a phenomenon than as so many independent and mutually exclusive kinds of scriptural knowledge.
>
> —H. S. Bhattacharya, *Reals in the Jaina Metaphysics*, Bombay, 1966, p p. 300-301

Sruta is virtually synonymous with *agama pramana* noted earlier. It may be conventional (*laukika*) or transcendental (*lokottara*). It may be pure text (*sutra*), commentsry (*artha*), or both (*sutrartha*).

Another classification of *agama pramana* is as *atmagama* (for the *tirthankaras*), *anantaragama* (for the *ganadharas*) and *paramparagama* (for the lay followers). These meanings are based on import (*artha*). On the basis of texts (*sutras*), the meanings would respectively be: for the *ganadharas*, for the immediate followers and for followers after the first generation.

INFERENCE

One of the sources of knowledge cited by Mahavira is inference (*anumana*). Inference is that kind of valid knowledge which is determinant of what is to be proved (*sadhya*) arising from some sign or external mark (*linga*) and standing in the relation of invariable concomitance (*vyapti*) with the same.

Such being the typical indication of inference in the Jaina view, it sets aside, on the one hand, the Buddhistic view which maintains that non-perception, identity and causality are the grounds of inference, and the Naiyayika view, on the other hand, which includes effect, cause, conjunction, co-existence, opposition, analogy, *apriori*-ness and *aposteriori*-ness in inference.

In the Jaina view, inference may be for one's own sake (*svarthanumana*) or for the sake of others (*pararthanumana*). Inference for one's own sake is valid knowledge arising in one's own mind from repeated observation of facts and corresponds to the first form of Aristotle's syllogism:

> All smoke is fire.
> The mountain smokes.
> Therefore, the mountain is on fire.

Inference for the sake of others is a statement expressive of reason (*hetu*) or middle term standing in relation of invariable concomittance with what is to be proved (*sadhya*) or major term, having been composed of the minor term (*paksa*). To be more precise, the minor term is defined to be that with which the major term is related, and whose relation with the major term is to be demonstrated. The major term stands for what is to be proved, and the middle term cannot stand without being in relation to the major term. To illustrate:

> The hill (minor term) is full of fire (major term) because
> it smokes (middle term).

Whatever is full of smoke, e.g., a kitchen, has fire (example)
The hill is full of smoke (application).
Therefore, the hill is on fire (conclusion).

The above illustration has five members, viz., major term, middle term, example, application and conclusion, and is considered to be mediocre. The bad type will have less than five members. The best exposition will have ten which are, the above five and their corrections.

The *Pramana Mimansa* contains the definition of the five members of the syllogism which are as follows:

> *Thesis is the statement of the theme to be proved.*
> *Statement of a probans ending in an inflexion unfolding is called reason.*
> *Example is the statement of an illustration.*
> *Application is the act of bringing the probans into connection with the minor term.*
> *Conclusion is the predication of the probandum.*

The five-membered and the ten-membered syllogisms are accepted in Jainism because they are useful to ordinary people who have no grounding in logic. They are also useful in removing the doubt in the mind of a person who may be listening to the argument. The ten-member syllogism is the earlier of the two, and there is reason to believe that it must have been due to the Jaina logicians.

DIRECT KNOWLEDGE

Direct knowledge is also called extra-sensory perception because it involves no use of any of the organs of senses or of mind. Its three forms are clairvoyance (*avadhi*), telepathy (*manah-paryaya*) and supreme (*kevala*).

The Jaina view of direct knowledge is easily understandable from their theory that the organs of senses and the mind are the limitations on the soul's power to know and see things straight. Only when they are made redundant and *karma* enshrouding knowledge and vision are removed, the soul is capable to attain the supreme and unobstructed knowledge and vision.

The *Bhagavati Sutra* and other texts are full of examples of *avadhi* knowledge of the gods, of infernal beings, of human beings and other beings with a developed reason. The objects coming within its scope are things which have shape, colour and extension. Formless things such as soul, motion, rest, space and time do not come within its range. It is the first of the extra-sensory perceptions, and has its corresponding ignorance called *vibhanga*.

Avadhi knowledge may be of three types, viz., *desavadhi*, *paramavadhi* and *sarvavadhi*. The range of the first is limited by spatial and temporal conditions. The range of the second is not limited by spatial and temporal conditions. The third one is the faculty by which we may perceive the non-sensuous aspects of all material things in the universe. *Desavadhi* has further divisions into congenital (*bhavapratyaya*) and acquired (*gunapratyaya*). The latter may be acquired by all beings who have the mind, and is due to the destruction or subsidence-in-part of the obstacles that hinder this form of knowledge. The former is a natural capacity in the celestial beings and in the infernal beings.

Manah-paryaya stands for a man's capacity to directly apprehend the thought in the minds of others. In the Jaina view, mind is made of subtle matter, and hence it is possible to apprehend its modes. In comparison with the *avadhi* knowledge which is to be found in all the existences, manah-paryaya is restricted to the human existence only. The *Nandi Sutra* gives the conditions under which this power comes to a man. They are full attainments (*paryapti*), right outlook (*samyak dristi*), perfect self-control and possession of extra-ordinary powers. There are two types of *manah-paryaya* knowledge which are *rijumati* and *vipulamati*, the former being lesser in purity, range and duration than the latter. The important points of difference between *avadhi* and *manah-paryaya* have been noted by S. Gopalan to be as follows:

	avadhi	manah-paryaya
Purity	Perception of material object and even mind is possible but it may not be very clear.	Perception of material object as well as of mind is clear.
Scope	Infinite degrees are possible from the perception of the minutest part of space to its limits.	It is limited to the sphere of human beings.

Subject	Possible for all living beings and in all forms of existence.	Possible only for men and only after registering some spiritual progress.
Objects	Limited to material objects; not all the infinite number o modes are perceived.	Extends to even minutest parts.

—S. Gopalan, *Outlines of Jainism*, New Delhi, 1973, p. 107

The Jaina philosophers are unanimous that there is one and only one form of knowledge which is immediate and most direct, and without which no one can be perfected, enlightened and liberated. This is *kevala jnana* or supreme and unlimited knowledge of the soul which is not restricted in any way by the barrier of space and time. The *kevala jnana* has been defined by the author of the *Tattvartha Sutra* to be full, complete, uncommon, absolute, pure, comprehensive, extensive over space as well as non-space, and infinite as a category. The superiority of *kevala jnana* over all others is brought out in the following manner: the objects of *mati* and *sruta* are substances but not in all their aspects; the objects of *avadhi* are again material substances in more aspects but not in all; the objects of *manah-paryaya* are the same as those of *avadhi* knowledge, but here knowledge is purer and more subtle; but the objects of *kevala jnana* are all substances in all their aspets. On a question by Indrabhuti Gautama on the absolute knowledge of the omniscient person, Mahavira said, in part, as follows:

> The omniscient knows the limited as well as the unlimited ... till his vision is without cover. So he does not take the help of organs of senses in order to know and see.
> —*Bhagavati Sutra*, S. 5, U. 4

Throughout the *Agamas*, notably the *Bhagavati Sutra*, there is ample proof of Mahavira's omniscience.

KNOWLEDGE IN A NUT-SHELL

At a later period, under the influence of other systems of Indian philosophy in which direct and immediate (*pratyaksa*) knowledge

6

is one which is derived from sense contact, notably the contact of the eye (*aksi*), the Jainas have slightly modified their stand without making any compromise regarding their original position. The modified Jaina view may be given in a nut-shell as follows:

avadhi, manah-paryaya and *kevala*	truly direct
sruta	indirect
mati derived through five organs of senses	truly indirect, but direct for practical purposes (*laukika pratyaksa*)
mati derived through mind	indirect

IN THE previous chapter, we have said that *srutas* may be of two types, viz., *naya sruta* and *syadvada sruta* according as they emphasize the particular or the total. *Naya srutas* teach us the ways of comprehending things and realities in their particular aspects. *Syadvada srutas*, in contrast, teach us the ways of comprehending things and realities in all their aspects. There are, of course, many bad *srutas* given by the heretics, but they are not deserving of our attention. *Naya srutas* and *syadvada srutas* together constitute words or testimony given by the seers.

Since in Mahavira's time, there were 363 philosophical schools centred round Jaina doctrines alone, it would have been acrimonious for any sensible person to reject them all in toto. Mahavira also did not do that. All the same, he did not say that anyone of these gave the whole truth. *Naya* and *syad* were tools for the purpose, and they were very intelligent tools indeed. Besides, they were original, since no other school of Indian philosophy could produce such helpful tools of toleration for rival viewpoints. *Syadvada* in particular, also called *anekantavada*, has relevance at any time and in any situation in which diverse view-points prevail.

Between Chapters 12, 13 and 14, there is a good deal of overlapping, and the intelligent reader is expected to understand what is what, and not to take the break-up of the chapters in a rigid sense.

NAYAVADA

According to the Jainas, there are many things and realities in the universe each having many attributes, and these, in turn, entering into many relations, so that it is not possible to affirm anything absolutely. All affirmations that we make in daily life are true only under certain conditions, and when conditions change, the affirmations cease to hold good. *Naya* is the instrumentality which recognises not only the plurality of things and realities, but also their infinite attributes and relations. As such, it helps us to go deep into the network of inter-related parts or attributes of a reality, take up one or the other, and interpret it or understand it with the idea of getting a correct and analytical view of its ontology. Hence, some writers have called *nayavada* as the doctrine of 'relative pluralism'. But though the emphasis in the *naya* theory is on one part or attribute, it is no denial of other parts or attributes, which may, likewise, be separately taken up for observation or consideration. There are two forms of *naya*, one called noumenal (*dravyar-thika*), and the other called phenomenal (*paryayarthika*), and the two together have seven forms as follows:

1. *Naigana naya* or the standpoint of the universal—particular: This is a combination of the universal (*samanya*) and the particular (*visesa*) attributes of a reality with stress evenly divided. The proposition, 'I am a human being', stresses the particularity of the speaker as a person as much as it does on the generality of his being a human being. It should, however, be noted that the Jainas made no synthesis between the two, nor held each to be absolute, but maintained each relatively to the other. According to the Jainas, therefore, those, who like the Nyaya-Vaisesika system, drew absolute distinction between the universal and the particular were victims of a fallacy called *naigama-nayabhasa*.

Naigama naya has also been used to state, on the basis of earlier acts, what is to follow next, without committing a fallacy. If a man carries water, rice and fuel, and when asked, says, he is cooking, he is perfectly justified; for, his preparation is controlled by a purpose or teleology which is cooking.

2. *Samgraha naya* or the standpoint of the universal: Without denying the complex nature of reality, the emphasis here is on the universal alone, and this is perfectly logical. But a fallacy is committed by the Sankhya and the Advaita schools, because in calling everything *sat*, they deny what is *asat*. *Asat* may for the time being be kept aside, but to deny it wholly is to commit a fallacy called *samgraha-nayabhasa*.

3. *Vyavahara naya* or the standpoint of the particular: If it be logical to extricate the universal as under item 2, it should be logical in the same way to extricate the particular from the amalgam without denying the universal. This is no fallacy. But a fallacy is committed, as has been done by the Carvakists, if the particular or the empirical alone is made an absolute item. The fallacy is called *vyavahara-nayabhasa*.

The three nayas described above, that of the universal-parti-cular, that of the universal and that of the particular, are the outcome of looking at the identity of things, and hence emphasise on the substance aspect of reality. In other words, they are noumenal. The remaining four that follow, which are based on modes, belong to the category of phenomenal *nayas*.

4. *Rjusutra naya* or the standpoint of momentariness: Here, only the present form of reality is important, not those that lie buried in the past, nor those that will emerge in the future; and when the emphasis is on the present, this present is no bigger than a point on a vast canvas of time. This is even not as big as the empirical-particular from which the idea of momentariness is but an 'extraction'. But, as always, the Jaina stand is relative, not absolute, and involves no fallacy. An actor who acts as a king on the stage is king for the time he acts, but neither before nor after, and to call him so is improper. When the fallacy is commited, it becomes *rjusutra-nayabhasa*.

5. *Sabda naya* or the standpoint of the synonyms: When two words convey the same meaning, we call them synonyms, but their letter composition is far from identical. Again, two words may refer to the same person, e.g., Indra, Sakra, Purandara, but they mean different achievements on the part of the same person. A fallacy is committed if two words conveying identical meaning are called identical in all respects, or different implications of two proper nouns referring to the same person are lost sight of. The fallacy is called *sabda-nayabhasa*.

6. *Samabhirudha* naya or the standpoint of etymology: To avoid the aforesaid fallacy in synonyms, the Jainas have used the etymological standpoint which emphasizes dissimilarities between words in their construction as well as their implication. Obviously, etymology is important, and to overlook it is to overlook difference not only between synonyms but also between non-synonyms. But an exclusive emphasis on etymology is as much fallacious as that on synonyms, and in treating these two as complementary, the Jainas have carefully avoided the fallacy called *samabhirudha-nayabhasa*.

7. *Evambhuta naya* or such-like standpoint: It is a sort of corol-lary from (6). The word *evambhuta* means 'true in its entirety',

i.e., in words as well as in meaning. Thus in *evambhuta naya*, the emphasis is not only on words, but also on implication. When this is lost sight of, it is a fallacy called *evambhuta-nayabhasa*.

The last four *nayas* may be re-stated as follows:

Rjusutra naya: Indra is the lord of the gods.
He becomes Sakra at the moment when he is displaying his prowess.
He becomes Purandara at the moment when he is destroying the enemies.

Sabda naya: The three words, Indra, Sakra and Purandara, by accepted implication, refer to one and the same person.

Samabhirudha naya: Etymologically, each of the three words have different composition. Their implications also are not identical.

Evambhuta naya: This is true to etymology as well as to meaning. Etymology is provided by the form of the three words, and the three refer to the different activities of the same person.

In their characteristic way to be too logical, the Jaina logicians have identified a hundred forms of each *naya* giving a total of 700. Some logicians have, however, accepted them to be six, knocking out the first, while some others have made them five by merging the sixth and the seventh in the fifth.

Nayavada stands for the logic of consistency.

SYADVADA

Our knowledge derived with the help of the ordinary arteries have three defects. First, in this, we cannot get rid of the material or sensuous origin of knowledge which consequently tends to betray the mind into illusion and error. Second, such knowledge must fail to give the real or organic connection and unity to objects which it deals with. And third, it is incapable of solving contradictions or reconciling the seemingly antagonistic elements which, on close scrutiny, all thoughts are found to contain.

And when we rise from the commonplace things of the world to the higher things of the spirit, it becomes necessary to apprehend objects which are no longer self-identical units, but each of which is, so to say, itself and other than itself. In such a state, we cannot affirm without at the same time denying, nor can we deny without at the same time affirming. Thus when seeming contradictions interpenetrate, and give reality and life to each other, the resources of the ordinary virtually dry up, and we have to look for some other mode of cognition which is more synthetical and harmonising. This new mode of cognition is called *sapta-bhangi naya, syadvada* or *anekantavada* which helps us to detect the unity which belongs to all things. In other words, this new tool is an expression of one underlying principle contributing to the substantiveness of all thoughts and beings.

Sapta-bhangi naya syadvada is the logic of unity in difference. The emphasis of *syadvada* is on unity in things and realities. Etymologically, the word *syat* is the subjunctive form of the root *as* (to be), so that *syadvada* becomes the doctrine of 'to be', or as it has been called, the doctrine of 'may be'. The implication is that no single proposition can express the whole of a thing or a reality in its entirety, since the thing or the reality consists of many attributes which, in turn, enter into many relations, and to be logically infallible, the attack must be launched from as many as seven angles, though regarding any one of them, we may say, 'may be'. Surendranath Dasgupta explains the significance of the expression 'may be' as follows:

> The truth of each affirmation is ... only conditional, and inconceivable from the absolute point of view. To guarantee correctness, therefore, each affirmation should be preceded by the phrase *syat* or 'may be'. This will indicate that the affirmation is only relative, made somehow, made from some point of view, and under some reservations, and not in any sense absolute. There is no judgement which is absolutely true and no judgemen which is absolutely false. All judgements are true in some sense and false in another.
> —S. N. Dasgupta, *A History of Indian Philosophy*, Cambridge University Press, 1963, Vol. 1, p. 179

That in *syadvada* there is a definite, unified view of reality is often missed by the critics. The significance of having as many as seven propositions is also not much appreciated by them. In the expression 'may be', they see a kind of scepticism which lands the Jainas into the situation of no view at all. But this is not correct. What the critics do not realise, or refuse to realise, is that the Jainas have a very definite view of reality which is that *no definite view of reality can be taken*, and seven propositions together, and not any one of them in isolation, can give insight into the nature of it.

Thus *syadvada* becomes complementary to *nayavada*, and what starts as the logic of consistency end up as the logic of identity. *Naya* is just an analytical tool, while *syat* is synthesis, different propositions extending hands to help the comprehension of the reality. The seven-fold propositions are as follows:

> *Syat asti dravyam*—may be, reality is.
> *Syat nasti dravyam*—may be, reality is not.
> *Syat asti ca nasti ca dravyam*—may be, reality is and is not.
> *Syat avaktavyam dravyam*—may be, reality is indescribable
> *Syat asti ca avaktavyam dravyam*—may be, reality is, and it is indescribable.
> *Syat nasti ca avaktavyam dravyam*—may be, reality is not, and it is indescribable.
> *Syat asti ca nasti ca avaktavyam dravyam*—may be, reality is and is not, and it is indescribable.

In a limited sense, any object in the world, is a reality, and the most popular object with the Jaina logicians is a *ghata* or an earthen pot. Now, we have to apply the seven propositions as above to the earthen pot.

Proposition one affirms the existence of a pot. But this in itself is not enough. In giving his definitive view to Skandaka Parivrajaka, Mahavira laid down that everything, every reality, a pot or the universe, has to be stated as substance, as time, as place and as mode or phenomenon. Coming back to our own example, the substance in the pot is mud. It exists at a particular place, and at a particular time, and that too in a particular shape, not at another place, at another time and not in any other form or shape. So long as these four elements exist in this particular combination, the pot is said to exist there as such. When the proposition emphasizes the elements, it is noumenal; when it emphasizes the qualities, e.g., size, shape, colour, taste and touch, it is phenomenal.

Proposition two does not contradict the first. It simply affirms that the pot does not exist. In the first proposition, we took the pot in the light of a self-identical unit. But this is only a partial and dogmatic view of the reality because it overlooks an important truth which is that the world is a system of interrelated parts in which nothing is so self-identical, self-complete, as we suppose the pot to be. Everything exists only in relation to and distinction from something else. The pot exists there, not alone as a self-complete reality, but in relation to and distinction from what is not-pot. In fact, the existence of the pot as a self-complete unit is possible only because it differentiates from what is not-pot. If, on the other hand, it looses its distinction and merges in the rest that is not-pot, then the pot cannot present its own self-subsisting and identical character. We may, therefore, well state that because it keeps itself in distinction from what is not-pot, and yet bears an essential relation to it as the principle of mutual reciprocity postulates that it can lead a life of self-completeness or self-identity. But this self-completeness cannot be absolute because it has to depend for its existence upon other things from which it distinguishes itself and yet stands in essential and vital relationship. In other words, a pot is a pot only in contradiction with what is not-pot, expressing a vital relationship between the positive and negative character of it co-existing simultaneously in the same stroke of cognition of the thing in question and making way thereby for the third proposition which follows.

Proposition three affirms that somehow the pot exists and does not exist as well. This may be explained from two different standpoints. First, if we proceed from the world showing it to be a system in which everything is determined by everything else in such a way that nothing is self-identical, it will be found that everything is determined by other things, and when this is accepted, the doctrine of pluralism propounding the view of self-sufficiency of objects falls. Second, the proposition may be explained in a way which throws light on the close relationship which exists between self and not-self, between mind and matter. The second standpoint in terms of mind and matter rather than in terms of the usual pot given a better explanation of this proposition.

In this world of ours, we have mind and we have matter, and matter is matter and mind is mind, and there is no similarity nor commensurability between the two. Attempts by other schools to establish a relation between the two have been futile. For, while the materialists have given exclusive emphasis on matter leading to naked empiricism, the dualists of the Sankhya type have placed the two in opposition. The real solution, as given by the Jainas, lies not in asserting self-individuality and self-sufficiency of objects constituting the external world but in surrendering the false identity in favour of an organic unity. Matter in its very essence is related to the mind and mind in its very essence is related to the matter. The true view of anything would be not only its being but also its not-being. In other words, a right view would include not only a view of things in their positive aspect, or as thesis, but also a view of things in their negative aspect, or an antethesis. And these lose their hard distinction and opposition because they are necessarily related, containing and involving one another. In this proposition, one has the genesis of the dialectic method of reasoning.

Proposition four refers to the indescribable nature of the pot. This means that we cannot describe what it is and what it is not at one and the same moment, and this is so because two natures, positive and negative, exist in the same thing at one and the same time. The positive is emphasized in the first proposition and the negative in the second, and in the third we find that it shelters both the positive and the negative, and now, the fourth which states that we cannot describe them in one moment (though we may have the cognition of the two at one and the same time in our thought).

The rest of the propositions become easy. The fifth proposition takes into consideration the existence and the indescribable nature at the same time. The sixth proposition takes into consideration the non-existence and the indescribable nature at the same time. The seventh and last proposition stands as a synthesis of propositions five and six.

UNITY IN DIFFERENCE

The entire doctrine of *syadvada* with its emphasis on the positive and negative is based on a dialectic reason which leads to the doctrine of unity in difference (*bhedabheda*). With the Jainas, everything implies that there is something opposed to it, the tenor of the argument being that everything is real in relation to and distinction from every other thing. This being so, while emphasizing the law of identity, the Jainas have not denied the law of contradiction in absolute terms. Rather, they strive to impress on us that distinction presupposes a unity of which soul and non-soul, virtue and vice and so on are but *prima facie* opposite expressions. This unity is all-inclusive which embodies everything that is real.

Here arises a fundamental controversy in philosophy. This is about the fundamental unity for which the word is 'absolute'. Now, if absolute is one, it is not many; if it is unity, it is not plurality. The Vedantists uphold unity but decry plurality which is the world on the ground that it is a grand illusion (maya). But to give such a huge thing the name of illusion is not to explain it. The Jainas have not done such a thing. They have accepted the world in all its plurality, and starting from it, they have sought to arrive at the fundamental unity.

In the Jaina view, the absolute is the universal, not the abstract universal of formal logic, but concrete universal. The absolute expresses itself in x but it is not limited to x. It extends to y and z and so on. Thus x which is the particularisation of the universal goes beyond itself to y and z and so on, so that x, y, z, till n are immanently and vitally connected with one another. The Jainas are not shy of the particulars nor do they reject them as illusion; rather, their absolute reveals itself in the particulars of the world.

The world system is not alien to thought but an expression of it. The whole universe of things we see must need be ordered in perfect agreement with our cognitions. We are conscious of things as different and non-different at the same time. As effects or particulars, they are different, but in their causal or universal aspect, they are non-different.

Things are naturally of dual character. In our example of the pot, clay is the cause and pot is the effect. The pot is the particular state of being of the universal-causal which is clay. If the co-existence of the causal-universal with the effect-particular were not possible, then it would never have been possible for clay to exist in the form of the pot. From this follows a useful corollary that identity is not always the destruction of difference.

The position is that it is impossible to distinguish rigidly between cause and effect, between universal and particular. They are neither absolutely different nor absolutely non-different, but they stand in the relation of what may be called unity in difference (*bhedabheda*).

THE JAINAS have considered the mind to be an obstruction to the direct and immediate knowledge of the soul. This is linked up with two types of *karma* called *vedaniya* and *mohaniya*. So although they never cared to give a complete theory of psychology in modern sense of the term, the canonical texts have copious references to the working of the mental mechanism which are the inspiration behind this chapter.

On a point raised by Indrabhuti Gautama, Mahavira said,

> *Beings without mind are of four types, which are, infernal beings without mind, subhuman beings without mind, human beings without mind and celestial beings without mind.*
> —*Bhagavati Sutra*, S. 1, U. 2

Mind is an important and effective organ with human beings for good as well as evil.

Elsewhere in the *Bhagavati Sutra*, Mahavira says,

> *A being with mind sometimes binds karma enshrouding knowledge and sometimes he does not. A being without mind binds. One not-with-mind not-without-mind (i. e., omniscient person) does not bind. Like this is to be known of the six types of karma, karma enshrouding pleasure and karma giving life-span excepted. As to karma enshrouding pleasure, a being with mind binds and so does a being without mind, but one not-with-mind not-without-mind sometimes binds and sometimes does not bind. As to karma giving life-span, a being with mind and a being without mind sometimes bind and sometimes do not bind, but one not-with-mind not-without-mind does not bind.*

MIND

Among living beings, some are endowed with mind. They are called *sanji*. Those who are not endowed with mind are called *asanji*.

---

*M. L. Mehta's *Jaina Psychology* is a useful work on the subject.

Leaving aside the omniscient personalities who are with and without mind, the existence of mind in a being makes him more developed. With mind, a being enjoys the possession of sensation, apprehension, comprehension, cognition, understanding, memory, ideas, etc., etc., all of which are due to the mind.

In the cognition of self and its attributes, mind acts independently; but in perceiving objects of the external world, it works in co-operation with the five organs of senses.

In the Jaina view, mind is *no-indriya* and *anindriya*. The former word means that mind is a sense organ in a limited sense, and the latter word means that mind is not an organ of sense. In any case, the Jainas have conceded to mind a separate status, and considers it, when and where necessary as an independent organ.

Thus while, in the Jaina view, mind stands as a separate item, its recognition caused no special difficulty to them, as it did in some other schools of Indian philosophy. For, in the Jaina view, knowledge derived by sense perception is as much indirect as that derived by mind. This further means that in the Jaina view, the organs of senses as well as mind stand equally between the knower and the object of knowledge, and are hence a positive obstruction to direct knowledge by the soul.

There are three points of distinction between the organs of senses and mind. First, the organs of senses occupy particular sites in the body where they can be pointed out, but not so the mind. Second, the organs of senses are turned outward and perceive the external objects through some sort of direct contact (touch); but mind is turned both inward and outward. When it is turned inward, it does not take help from organs of senses, but when it is turned outward, it perceives external objects with the help of these organs. Third, each of the sense organs has specific objects to perceive, but mind is more pervasive and it has everything within its jurisdiction. It is capable of cognising all objects touched by all sense organs. This mind is capable of because it is a very subtle organ.

Hemacandra has given the most consistent definition of mind. According to him, mind is the organ of cognition of all objects of all the sense organs. This definition serves a two-fold purpose. First, it differentiates mind from other sense organs, and second, it differentiates mind from self. Had mind been an organ of direct

cognition, it would have been at par with self. But it is not that.
It is very much different from self, a positive obstruction to self's
direct knowledge. As to the distinction from other organs of senses,
mind helps these to cognise all objects. Thus mind rules over
the entire domain of the sense organs, and in the absence of it,
these would impart nothing to understanding. In the words of
the *Nandi Sutra,* mind is that which grasps everything.

In Hemacandra's definition, the emphasis is on the function
of mind. Mind is to be known from the function it discharges.
In recent years, some western psychologists have approached mind
from this angle. To understand mind, they say, we have to gather
all possible facts of human behaviour and experience and infer
from them the true nature and structure of mind.

In the Jaina view, mind is both physical and psychical, *dravya-
manah* and *bhava-manah.* Physical mind is made of very subtle
matter, for which it is also called material mind. A Jaina text
defines material mind as a collection of fine particles which are
meant for exciting the thought-process due to the activities arising
out of the contact of the soul with the body.

Psychical mind stands for mental processes. In the Jaina view,
the highest state is, of course, that where the soul regains its capacity
for direct knowledge without the aid of the sense organs or mind.
But that stage is not near at hand, and one has to go a long way
where, in early stages at least, the importance of the mental processes
cannot just be ignored. It is through the same mental process that
the self is rid of *karma* obstructing knowledge. This process which
improves the receptivity of mind is called *labdhi.* In addition to the
annihilation of *karma* obstructing knowledge, there is required
the positive modification of the self into conscious mental activity.
These two, the improvement in the receptivity of mind and the
positive modification of the self into conscious mental activity,
reciprocate one another and are basically the two aspects of the
same function of the mind. As H. S. Bhattacharya states:

> Internal conscious processes, e.g., comparison, concep-
> tion, etc., are impossible unless and until the conscious
> principle, the soul, is possessed of *labdhi,* i.e., the power
> of comparing, conceiving, etc. These internal processes
> are impossible again, unless and until there is upayoga,

unless and until, that is to say, there is some subjective effort (attention) to carry on these mental processes.
—H. S. Bhattacharya, *Real in the Jaina Metaphysics*,
Bombay, 1966, pp. 243-44

Thus mind is not simply the organ of all organs; it is also an instrument to attain a higher state of consciousness. As a Jaina text has put it,

> It is by the help of mind that one can learn, understand the gestures, receive instructions and follow conversation. . . . It is through mind that one is enabled to decide before doing what ought to be done and what ought not to be done. It is through mind, again, that one can learn the distinction between the real and the unreal.
> —*Gommatasara, Jiva-kanda*, 662

While the material constituent of mind has permanence, the modes which are responsible for the mental processes are ever changing, making mind the most restless of all the sense organs. It is this restlessness of mind that may lead one to perdition, and to save oneself from it, the first thing one is required to do is to establish a complete control over mind, to delimit the zone over which it moves and to reduce it steadily till the zone totally disappears. Left to itself, mind penetrates and trespasses into any part of the universe with a speed which is faster than the speed of light. We have it in the life of Mahavira that when he moved, he never looked to his sides or the rear, and even in his front, he never looked at an area bigger than the size of a man. And when he stood in some difficult posture in meditation, he pinned his mind at a point so that it would not stray at will. Mind is a good servant but a bad master. It is mind that helps one to attain higher conscious. It is like a ladder. But if it be given a free play, it is the most potent instrument for self-annihilation.

These days, a huge literature is coming from the west, particularly the United States, purported to interpret the mind. But their purpose is very restricted to the elementary plain of sensation and its measurement, effect of emotions on the outer physical body, etc., without bothering to investigate how the same mind can be turned into an effective instrument of attaining the highest perception. Despite its huge and ever-growing pile, however, the western psychology is without a conclusion and will never arrive at one, since every moment it reverts to the consciousness that there are as many minds as conscious beings, and as many as situations.

Mind has never been viewed in this manner in India by the Jaina or any other philosopher. In the Jaina view, the province of mind is 'the higher department of thought which seeks to understand the nature of things whose presence is the source of light and life in the body, and also of action and inhibition of action, and of the diversified impulsions and promptings of the mind.'

MENTAL PROCESSES

Although mind is made of matter, the matter particles are so very fine and subtle that they cannot be perceived by the organs of senses. It is this difficulty that led many ancient people to use the term 'soul' to indicate their conception of a knowing substance which is indivisible and indestructible. The Jainas, however, made no confusion. They have been ever alert about the distinction between soul and mind, and they have always considered mind as an obstacle to soul's direct knowledge.

Mind is, therefore, to be known from the mental processes for which a generic expression is 'perception'. Perception is taking into consciousness all things observed and all experiences undergone. Perception is to be distinguished from stimulus on the one hand and understanding on the other. Stimulus is caused by some external object, say, colour, sound, taste, smell or touch, and is material in nature; perception is a psychic process. When there is a stimulus, it calls forth perception. It has degrees and the highest perception is *kevala jnana*. At a lower stage, however, all living beings are endowed with two kinds of consciousness, viz., perception and understanding. Understanding relates to the import of what is perceived. Now, even the lowest form of life has these two, even though, in their case, they are difficult to distinguish from instinct. In the case of higher forms of life, instinct is replaced by a conscious process called volition.

Social scientists have three words to express men's volition, viz., 'want', 'desire' and 'demand'. In mental sciences, we have their analogues as 'impulse', 'desire' and 'will'. When impulse is less active, it is quiescent; when it is more active, it determines the line of thought and action for the individual. Then the impulse transforms into desire, which readily changes into will and activity. The character or disposition of an individual consists in the sumtotal of his desires, milder intensity and lesser number indicating a higher type and vice versa.

Desires, when not controlled, develop into passions called *kasayas*. The Jainas have identified four passions covering virtually all uncontrolled desires of the mind. They are anger, greed, deceit and pride. Each may assume four forms depending on the degree of intensity, which are, mild, strong, overwhelming and irresistible. A man who has harnessed himself to irresistible passions can do any rash thing, including suicide and homicide.

Like will, intellect also is a quality of the mind, and covers the thought aspect. The demarcation is not rigid. Will is sobered by intellect, as a violent will may overthrow intellect. But when the intellect is a victim of perversion or prejudice, the mind ceases to act rationally. Unfortunately, all men, as individuals and nations, are victims of some perversions and/or prejudices making an international community of human beings a very distant abstraction, almost a dream. So four passions plus prejudice, these five, act as limitations on the intellect or the thinking faculty of the mind. These are shown in the following diagram (see page 98).

It will be seen in the diagram that mind of an ordinary person is captivated by passions and prejudices which, in turn, have varying degrees of intensity. Only when these go out, the soul becomes free from its association with matter and is fit to be liberated.

Coming to a few other mental processes, attention is the instrument of conscious enquiry and of succession of perception and knowledge. Unless attention is directed to an object, it will not be duly cognised by the mind. Attention is another name for concentration, and depends on interest. It brings the object on which it is fixed into the limelight of consciousness.

Attention is not only an instrument of conscious enquiry, it is also an instrument of limitation of knowledge in so far as it shuts out objects on which attention is not given. Attention is also an instrument of succession in so far as we concentrate on diverse things not at a time, but one after another.

7

	greed	deceit	pride	anger	fanaticism	
irresistible	4	4	4	4	bigotry false conviction agnosticism	gross wickedness and ignorance
overwhelming	3	3	3	3	soul knowledge with strong love for bodily personality	faith with strong superstitions fear for bodily self
strong	2	2	2	2	soul knowledge with decreasing attachment for body	faith still tinged with superstition
mild	1	1	1	1	pure right faith	right faith freed from superstition
subdued passions: quiescent desires	....					advanced soul: right faith, knowledge and conduct
absence of	pure spirit bereft of matter					divinity: omniscience

—from C. R. Jain, *Jaina Psychology*

A living being is a bundle of impulses. When impulses become strong, they turn into instincts. Some of these instincts are as old as life, e.g., instinct of life itself, of food, of procreation. As a human instinct, accumulation or possession is very old. A *vitaraga* is one who has conquered even the primary instincts which are life itself. A *vitaraga* has no attachment to life, to food, to procreation or to possession.

Mind is an important instrument of decision-making, forecasting and projecting. These days, mechanical devices like computers have been devised to help the human mind in decision-making process; but computers have not been able to replace the human mind, which is considered to be the most powerful computer, and leaders of industry recognise no limitation on their mental ability to take decision on even the most difficult problems and issues.

The human mind, again, helps one in the process of recollection. This gives memory. It helps us to recall a thing or an event and also to reproduce it. It is because of memory that past can be recalled before our mind's eye. ... It is memory that helps man to store experience and benefit therefrom. A man without memory lives in the momentary present. Such a man is not very different from an animal.

Memory, like intellect, attention, etc., is a faculty of mind which is liable to increase or decrease through culture. There are people, notably recluses, who, by conscious effort, obliterate the memory of the past with a view to start life anew. There are people who use drugs to blunt the faculty of the mind. Again there are persons who enjoy the gift of a long memory and can in a way recall their previous life.

There are various other mental processes like association of ideas, dreams and visions, a train of thought, inhibition, pleasure and pain, emotion, etc. We omit details about them except for the last two items which are discussed below.

MIND AND KARMA

Mind is an instrument for good and evil because it itself is a victim of two types of *karma*, viz., *vedaniya* and *mohaniya*, and till these two exist, the efficacy of mind does not go.

Vedaniya karma is responsible for the feeling of pleasure and pain. Beings who have mind have the feeling of pleasure and pain. Those who have no mind have no feeling of pain. For instance, the infernal beings have no feeling of pain, not even of great pain (*maha-vedana*). This type of karma is thus responsible for feeling. *Mohaniya karma* obstructs right vision and right conduct. It generates delusion and creates emotions.

Pleasure is of three kinds and pain is of two kinds. Pleasures are physical, mental and spiritual; pains are physical and mental. Spiritual pleasure has no counterpart in pain.

In the Jaina view, passion is at the root of all feeling of pleasure and pain. There is nothing which is considered pleasure by all, nor so with pain. One man's sauce is another man's poison. This is so nicely brought out in the following:

> *Thus the objects of the senses and of the mind cause pain to passionate men, but they never in the least cause any pain to the dispassionate.* (100)
>
> *Pleasant things (by themselves) do not cause indifference nor emotions (as anger, etc.); but by either hating or loving them, a man undergoes such a change through delusion.* (101)
>
> *Anger, pride, deceit, greed; disgust, aversion to self-control and delight in sensual things (rati and arati); mirth, fear, sorrow, carnal desire for women, men or both; all these manifold passions arise in him who is attached to pleasures; and so do other emotions produced by those arise in him who is to be pitied, who (ought to be) ashamed of himself, and who is hateful.* (102-103)
>
> *A monk should not desire a companion, not (even) one who is able to perform his religious duties; nor, if he regrets having taken the vow, (should he desire for) a worldly reward for his austerities. Such emotions of an infinite variety arise in one who is the slave of his senses.* (104)
>
> *Desiring happiness and being submerged in the ocean of delusion, he forms many plans for warding off misery; and for their sake, an impassioned man exerts himself.* (105)
>
> *But all kinds of objects of the senses, sounds, etc., will cause to the indifferent neither a pleasant nor an unpleasant feeling.* (106)
>
> — *Uttaradhyayana Sutra* (Jocobi's translation)

Feelings of pleasure and pain touch the mind through the body, but emotions are more complex because they have a straight impact on the mind. Emotions result in acts of various kinds which, in turn, entangle man more and more into the shackles of life's varied experiences. Since emotions differ in intensity, the bondage is also varied. The Jaina philosophers make use of the term *lesya* to indicate the closely-knit pattern resulting from the mingling of passion and action. In explaining *lesya*, H. v. Glasenapp writes,

According to the moral value of their activity—and corresponding also to the kind of *karma* which they bind—the *jivas* can be divided into six categories. . . . The appertainment to one of these 6 classes shows itself in the soul externally; the soul which is free by nature from all distinctions perceptible by the senses receives colour, smell, taste and touch; in short, it becomes a defined type . . . although in a manner not recognisable by our senses.

—Helmuth von Glasenapp,
The Doctrine of Karma, Bombay, 1942, p. 47

SELF AS SUBJECT

Various mental processes delineated above, which are the outcome of *karma* and are purely subjective in the Jaina view, would not have been possible but for the existence of a subject. This subject is the self, for which another name is soul. The subject is not only endowed with consciousness, it is also eternal and permanent. The essential characteristic of self is consciousness which distinguishes the living from the non-living and the dead. Even when a living being is asleep, and fast asleep, he is not devoid of consciousness. For, otherwise, he cannot recall the pleasant experience of having a sound sleep. The self is also permanent, living through eternity, and not merely 'a bundle of experiences' as in Buddhism.

The self has been variously described in the Jaina texts. According to the author of *Nyayavatara*, the self is the knower; it illumines itself as well as others; it is the doer and enjoyer, the changing, it is proved by its own self, consciousness. This self is different from the elements. Eleswhere, it is stated that the self is the master, the doer, the enjoyer; though encased in the body, it is incorporeal. As a potter considers himself the maker and enjoyer of the pot, so, from practical view-point, the self or the soul in worldly life is the doer of things like constructing the body in which the self resides and enjoying the sense objects which are scattered all around him.

Once Indrabhuti Gautama cited some heterodox views regarding the existence or otherwise of the soul to Mahavira with a view to eliciting his considered views, whereon Mahavira said in part as follows:

> Goyama ! The self is indeed directly cognisable to you also. Your knowledge about it which consists of doubts, etc., is itself the self. What is proved by your own experience should not be proved by other means of knowledge. ... The self is directly experienced owing to ahampratyaya— the realisation as 'I' in 'I did', 'I do' and 'I shall do',— the realisation which is associated with the functions pertaining to all the three terms. ... If the object about which one has doubt is certainly non-existent, who it is that has the doubt whether I do exist or I do not exist? Or, Goyama, when you yourself are doubtful about your self, what can be free from doubt. ... The self which is the substratum of its attributes is self-evident owing to the attributes being self-evident, as is the case with a pot. For, on realising the attributes, the substratum, too, is realised.
>
> —*Visesavasyaka-bhasya*, 1554-58.

THE DIALECTIC of syadvada considered earlier provides the basis not only of Jaina ontology (*jiva-ajiva, akasa-kala, dharma-adharma*) but also of Jaina ethics (*papa-punya, asrava-samvara, vedana-nirjara*). But unlike the Hegelian dialectic which was used by Karl Marx in formulating his famous theory of the overthrow of capitalism, which has now been harnessed by the neo-Marxists like Herbert Marcuse to prepare a grand doctrine of 'perpetual revolution' in human society, the Jaina dialectic is not something perpetual, but terminates with the attainment of *moksa* by the individual soul, which is the *summum bonum* of human life.

Ontology which is another name for metaphysics is devoted to the consideration of the real or reals. It has been the unanimous finding of all the God-centred religions that God is the only real, God transcendental more than God immanent, so that everything else is unreal, a mere illusion or falsehood, or a manifestation of the will of the real, with a possibility of winding up when the real so desires. The problem has not bothered atheists like Carvakists to whom empirical is real; or the Buddhists to whom nothing, not even the soul, is bigger than a moment; or perhaps their modern counterpart, the existentialists. None of these have bothered about the distant abstraction called God. Nor have the Jainas; but unlike others in the God-centred religions, the Jainas have bothered much about the universe whose components are their reals, and these components do not depend on the will of anybody, but exist in their own right from an eternal past and will continue to a non-ending future. In this universe, the Jainas emphasize, of which the souls are a component, these souls are the veritable Godheads, though at this moment, their Godly attributes lie buried under a thick coat of matter. But with right effort, they may regain their Godliness, which does not mean going out of the universe to merge in some imaginary transcendental being, but moving to the crest of the sphere, and remaining there stationed for all times in perfect bliss and happiness.

---

* K. K. Dixit's *Jaina Ontology* is an useful study on this subject. Its focus is on the age of *Agamas* and the Age of Logic.

COMPARATIVE METAPHYSICS

The following gives a bird's-eye view regarding the position of different schools of Indian philosophy on the question of real with Advaita Vedanta of Sankara standing at one end and Buddhism standing at the other:

Pure unity	*Difference*
Advaita: Brahman as Reality, Universe an illusion.	*Vaisesika:* emphasizes *visesa* or differences.
Sankhya: Though dualistic, Prakrti represents only the *samsthanabheda* of Purusa, and is not independent.	*Dvaita:* Individual Souls differentiated from Universal Soul, the former being 'not that'.
Qualified unity	
Visista Advaita: Brahman a complex whole which incorporates within itself unity as well as difference	*Buddhism:* Moments alone are real, and continuity is a sham.

The word *advaita* means non-dualism, identity or, what we have called unity. According to the Advaita Vedanta, Brahman, which is a word for a transcendental God, is the one, exclusive, ultimate reality, everything else, including our own world and ourselves being no more than phenomena. The plurality or difference that we see around us give us no idea of reality because our consciousness is enshrouded by nescience. If nescience could be wiped out with the help of science which Vedanta is, then, we may stand face to face with reality.

The leading exponent of Advaita Vedanta is Sankara, a great name among reformers of Hinduism. He is said to have erected four bulwarks and rescued Hinduism from the corrupting influence of the Tantra-mixed Buddhism. Others have considered Sankara to be a hidden Buddhist. We are not interested in what he was, but in his view on the question of reality. Sankara's conception of the universe is based upon his theory of *vivrta* or the appearance of the real into something which it is not, to illustrate which he uses the analogy of a rope, which appears like a snake to an ignoramus, but as a rope to the enlightened person. Extending this analogy to the universe, Sankara would say the universe appears as real to the ignoramus, but, to the truly enlightened, Brahman is the only reality. Thus, Sankara's ontology is a pure, homogeneous unity.

The Sankhya school introduces two items, *Purusa* and *Prakrti*, which would create the impression that in this view, reality is dual. Of these two, *Purusa* is conscious though effectually dormant, and *Prakriti*, though unconscious, is dynamic. It is the latter that is the agency for all changes and all phenomena in the universe. In this view, therefore, evolution tends to differentiation, like the opening of petals of a flower when it blossoms, while dissolution leads to unity again, as it happens to a flower whose petals close after blossom throughout the day. The effect is contained in the cause, and is neither separate from, nor independent of, it. In the Sankhya view, therefore, despite its dynamism, *Prakrti* is subservient to the dormant *Purusa*, who alone is consciousness and activates the unconscious.

Visista Advaita stands for a qualified non-dualism of which the exponent has been Ramanuja. While in the Advaita view, difference is completely obliterated by unity because difference is unreal, according to Ramanuja, difference is not a mere mental construction, nor is it obliterated by unity; it comes to rest in an abiding unity, or it gets integrated with an enduring unity. Thus, in this view, difference does not stand rejected; it merely becomes an adjective of Brahman.

The Vaisesika view is so called because its emphasis is on *visesa* or difference which is one of the six realities, other five being substance, quality, activity, generality and intimacy. In the list of six, *visesa* stands fifth; and if still the school is named after the fifth item, and not the first, it shows the overwhelming importance in which difference is held. But the difference is not total; it is modified by the sixth item which is intimate relation.

Although the Dvaita school apparently stands for pure dualism, one of the two, the universe, is the dependent item, leaving God alone as the only independent item. But the difference between the two is stated to be basic, so that the dependent item is expressed as that which is not independent. To the question, what the soul is, an exponent of this school would say, 'it is not that'. Such is their 'great word' which differentiates the Individual Soul from the Universal Soul.

The Buddhist view holds nothing real, neither unity nor difference, but emphasizes on soullessness, impermanence and misery. Notions like soul, eternality, bliss which one comes across in the *Upanisads*, are alien to the Buddhist terminology. 'What is identical or similar is not ultimately real'—this is the Buddhist view expressed in a few words. Being is replaced wholesale by becoming. The only reals are the 'moments', but they do not last, making each point in existence to be entirely autonomous and independent.

JAINA METAPHYSICS

Bhante ! kim tattvam
(What is the nature of reality?)

In giving his considered view on the above question by Indrabhuti Gautama, Mahavira said,

'Origination'.

When the question was repeated twice, Mahavira gave out two more words:

'Destruction', 'Permanence'

This, in brief, is the Jaina view. The tone is set by *syadvada*. Reality is neither unity alone, nor difference alone, but unity in difference. In the Jaina view, all schools have stated only a grain of truth, but not the absolute truth. Absolute truth can be given only by an omniscient personality who can look at things straight.

Forms come up every moment, but this is no genesis or creation; forms go out to take new forms again, but this is no destruction or deluge. It is only a change of form. At the base of every change, there is a permanent base on which the change operates or become effective. This base consists of two items, the very first in the dialectic, *jiva* and *ajiva*, consciousness and not-consciousness, which stand not juxtaposed, but in complete harmony and co-existence from an eternal time. This unity in difference is the universe.

The universe taken as one, undivided whole must be increate, eternal, self-existent and ever-permanent. But viewed from the standpoint of its inter-related parts, it is transitory, phenomenal and evanascent. This assertion of a self-existent universe is simply an indirect denial not only of creation, but also of an extra-cosmic personality who builds cosmos out of chaos. The universe as a whole or in part is but permutations and combinations of four reals, viz., space, time, soul and matter. These reals are resolvable into the minutest of their minute parts which set a limit to fresh divisions by not admitting of any further analysis. Even according to modern science, the universe is nothing more than an ever changing permutations and combinations of atoms, molecules and cells forming the character and composition of the same. But while modern science adequately explains how these changes are effected, it is incapable to explain why these changes are effected.

The reason why modern science cannot answer the point in question is that it takes only a partial view of things and does not look straight to the principles of causation. We have stated that the universe is a system of inter-related parts, and the parts, as such, are conditioned. But things conditioned must be the effect of something which is the cause. The cause is two-fold, viz., substantial and determining or efficient, called 'patient' and 'agent' in European logic. In our example of the pot, the substantial cause is the clay, which is turned into a pot by the potter with the help of some equipments, which, in consequence, become the determining cause. The distinction is very important; for, it is the determining cause, operating on the substantial cause, that accounts for the differences in things.

ASTI-KAYAS

According to the Jaina view, a proper understanding of reality consists in comprehending both *jiva* and *ajiva*, consciousness and not-consciousness, and not in leaving any one of these out of account, nor in calling one or the other unreal. Since this has not been done in other schools, they contain only a relative truth.

In the Jaina view, real is not different from the hard core of reality which is existence itself. The emphasis on taking into consideration both conscious and not-conscious aspects into reality leads to a position in which soul, matter, space, time, motion and rest,—all become reals. Leaving aside soul which alone is conscious, the remaining five are forms of not-consciousness or *ajiva* and the Jaina terms for them are *pudgala*, *akasa*, *kala*, *dharma* and *adharma*.

At one place in the *Bhagavati Sutra*, time is left out of account and it is stated that the universe is made of the remaining five items. Says Mahavira,

> *Goyama ! The universe is composed of five extensive substances, which are, the medium of motion, the medium of rest, space, soul and matter. (Sataka* 13)

From this it has been inferred by scholars that perhaps at Mahavira's time, there were two schools in Jainism, one including time in the list of reals and another excluding it. This does not appear to be a convincing view. For, the above quotation makes specific reference to 'extensive substances' only, and since time has never been considered to be extensive, its exclusion from the above quotation does not strike it off from the list of reals.

This brings us to an important concept which is typical of Jaina metaphysics, viz., the concept of *astikaya*. The words has two syllables, *asti* and *kaya*, the former standing for the state of being and the latter for the state of extensiveness. *Astikayas* are five, viz., soul or *jivastikaya*, matter or *pudgalastikaya*, space or *akasastikaya*, medium of motion or *dharmastikaya* and medium of rest or *adharmastikaya*. All of them exist, all have extensiveness and all are, therefore, real. All these are manifested in their changing modes and differing qualities.

Kala or time is also a real, though it is not an *astikaya*. It is because time is not extensive in space, though it is coeval with it. Even time has changing modes and differing qualities.

All the six items noted above have been considered to be substances or *dravyas*, since all the six exist, and all of them are capable of assuming different modes and exhibiting varying qualities. A typical Jaina definition of substance is:

> *That which maintains its identity while manifesting its various qualities and modification, and which is not different from satta, is called dravya.*   —*Pancastikaya,* 8

This being so, we arrive at a position where reals, reality, existence and substance become just interchangeable terms. What is the hard core of existence is reality, and what is reality is also existence. To call such a real thing as existence unreal, a falsehood, an illusion, is a distortion of truth. Reals in Jainism are neither a mental hallucination, nor a distant abstraction, but substance. As the *Tattvartha-sutra Bhasya* has laid down in a verse form:

All is one because all exist. (1.35)

Truly, a victory for *syadvada*, for the principle of unity in difference !

According to some scholars, although the older Agamas named the basic reals, they never attempted a definition of the term 'real' or of 'substance'. They hold further that the need for such definition arose at a time when the Brahmins and the Buddhists were engaged in a duel on these issues. According to them, the earliest such definition was attempted by Umasvati, who said that the real is something which is possessed of origination, destruction and permanence (*utpada-vyaya-dhrauvya-yuktam sat*). We have seen earlier that these three words are due to Mahavira himself. And as for definition of the real, we have the following in the *Bhagavati Sutra* in the words of Indrabhuti Gautama:

savvam atthi-bhavam atthi vadamo
savvam natthi-bhavam natthi vadamo

(That which exists shall I call an existing entity; That which does not exist shall I call a non-existing entity.)

There should, however, be no dispute on the point that the idea of *astikayas* may have been older than the *Bhagavati Sutra*, and it took some time to take shape. The earliest to come up must have been the idea of *loka* having a particular shape and size, and also that of an empty *aloka* surrounding *loka*. Naturally, the *loka* was taken to be the permanent seat of matter and soul. The remaining three concepts of *dharma*, *adharma* and *akasa* must have come up at a later period. Thus in a dialogue in the *Bhagavati Sutra*, it is maintained that a god standing at the far end of the *loka* cannot move about his limbs, not because there is no motion and rest in *aloka*, but because there is no matter there. This must have been the earlier position, but at a later period, the absence of media of motion and rest in *aloka* is specifically emphasized so that, it follows, the *loka* cannot trespass or intrude into *aloka*.

We have already the Jaina definition of substance. Two more related things are *pradesa* (space-point) and *payyaya* (property). All substances consist of space-points and have property. The space-points of *dharma*, *adharma* and *akasa* behave in one way, those of souls in another way and those of matter in a third way. Thus in the case of *dharma*, etc., one space-point must exist at a different place from another, and it must always exist where it is. In the case of souls, one space-point cannot coexist with any other, and they may change positions. In the case of matter, the space-points are its constituent atoms, and one space-point may co-exist with any number of such space-points, and they may change positions, as in the case of the souls; but, unlike the souls, in the case of matter, the space-points may transfer from one physical body to another, or may even remain loose.

The consideration of space-points gave the realisation that occupying a certain portion of space is an important feature of substance. There was a simultaneous realisation that occupying a certain portion of time should be another feature of substance; but there was difficulty, because this necessitated conceiving time, like space, as so many points. This was suitably done and the idea of *samaya* or a time-point came up. Thus while *kala* is time eternal, *samaya* stands for a point of time which is divisible no further. The *Bhagavati Sutra* has a complete division of time, from *samaya* as the minimum till *sagaropama* which is the maximum. With this new tool, it was now possible to conceive substance as occupying a portion of time, as small as one *samaya*.

Coming to *paryayas* or property of substance, it has been maintained that each *paryaya*, physical as well as mental, has an infinite number of degrees, from the smallest till the largest. With *dravya*, *pradesa* and *paryaya*, the *Agamic* ontology reached its acme of development. Combining the three, it may be stated that substance has four types of space points, viz., space-points viewed as substance, space-points viewed as place, space-points viewed as time and space-points viewed as property.

It was now clear that whatever exists is substance, and a substance may belong to any one of the following categories: *dharma*, *adharma*, *akasa*, *pudgala-paramanu* (molecules), *pudgala-skandha* (cluster) and *addha-samaya*. It was also clear that almost all types of substances are composites belonging to the following five categories:

(*i*)   *Dharma*, *adharma* and *akasa* are composites whose components remain fixed in location as well as in number.

(ii) A *jiva* is a composite whose components remain fixed in number but not in location.

(iii) A *pudgala-skandha* is a composite whose components are neither fixed in number nor in location.

(iv) A *pudgala-paramanu* is not a composite.

(v) *Addha-samaya* is not a composite.

Of the six substances, *jiva* stands for consciousness and has no form; *pudgala* has form but no consciousness; the remaining four have neither form nor consciousness. The *Bhagavati* contains a classification of these from the standpoint of form only, as *rupin* (with form) and *arupin* (without form), and includes only *pudgala* in the first category.

JIVA*

The Jaina system maintains that *jiva* or soul is a real and hence a substance. It is neither created nor can it be destroyed, so that it is eternal. There is an infinite number of souls, all imperceptible because all are formless. All souls are characterised by a consciousness which one does not come across in any other substance. It is because of this consciousness that soul (in a human body) is capable of acquiring not only *darsana* or general knowledge but also *jnana* or perception till the supreme knowledge, and even attaining *moksa*.

The Jainas developed a cosmographical gradation of souls which is more or less in agreement with those developed in other Indian systems. But the Jainas took a hylozoistic view of nature that there is nothing in the world of matter, nothing which exists in space and time which is not some form of *jiva*. And it is assumed that all of them are in the process of development or evolution in their physical structures, modes of generation, food and drink, ideas, knowledge, intelligence and the like. In consequence, we have in Jainism such forms of living organism as earth-bodies, water-bodies, air-bodies, fire-bodies and flora-bodies. Thus earth is not dead clay but consists of living organism called *prithvi-kaya*, water is not mere H_2O but *ap-kaya*, fire is *agni-kaya*, air is *vayu-kaya* and flora is *vanaspati-kaya*. The lowest of these are the material lives. The

---

* *Ajiva* which is the other item of the pair will be considered in part V, Chapters 23-25.

plants with their sub-species stand above material lives. From the plants, we pass on to the animal world consisting of an infinite variety of species, and from that to the world of men. Above and below are the celestial and infernal beings.

The Jainas have a distinction between liberated and non-liberated souls, the former being called the perfected beings or *siddhas*. The state of perfection is virtually attained in human life, and liberation comes at death, after which the soul, freed from all *karmic* matter is light enough to soar higher and higher, till it reaches the eternal abode of the perfected beings, *siddhasila*, at the crest of the sphere and slightly separated from it. *Siddhasila* is the goal of all souls as they are evolving through space and time, for in attaining this region, which is all freedom and bliss, the soul enters into *nirvana*. Liberation in the Jaina view is a spatial concept, viz., attaining the abode of the liberated souls at the crest of the sphere, and not merging in any imaginary thing called Absolute.

Leaving aside the perfected souls, all others are in one or the other of the four existences from an eternal time, and they are moving through them. The beauty and magnanimity of such a view-point is that it recognises the continuity of consciousness from the lowest of the animate beings to the highest, from which follows the corollary that whatever its stage, high or low, no *jiva* or soul is deserving of contempt or condemnation. The most logical outcome of this view is the Jaina doctrine of *ahimsa*. Consistent with the logic of continuity of consciousness, the Jaina theory insists on reverence for life.

The Jaina idea regarding the advent of different living beings in different states or forms of existence are on the whole similar to those held in other Indian systems. All of them believe in the trans-migration of soul, and the soul in Jainism, as in most of the Indian systems, is the factor which polarises the field of matter and brings about the organic combination of the elements of existence. If the position be that death means an event which takes place when the soul leaves the body, the question arises whether it passes off in some form of corporeality or not in any form of corporeality. The tradi-tional Jaina position is that with regard to gross body characterised by *audarika*, *vaikriya* and *aharaka*, the soul goes out without any corporeality, while with regard to the subtle body, characterised as *taijasa* and *karmana*, the soul departs in its subtle body.

The idea of transmigration of soul is all right in the various Indian systems, including the Jaina; but the point of interest is, why such a transmigration takes place. The *Sthananga Sutra* states six positions three of which are the outcome of bad deeds and three of good deeds. The first bunch of three due to bad deeds requiring another birth are as follows:

(*i*) bad deeds done during the present life require another life, which may be the life following, or life next to that;

(*ii*) bad deeds done in the last or previous life may bear fruit during the present life; and

(*iii*) bad deeds done in the last or previous life may not have borne fruit till now, and may not bear fruit in the rest of this life, and so may require another life. The same three forms may be repeated for good deeds, bearing in mind that good deeds are as much a bondage as the bad ones, and inserting the word 'good' in place of 'bad'.

Now, the point is, what is this 'another life'. Does it mean that the soul is moving from a lower stage of consciousness to a higher stage through some sort of evolution? Or, does it mean that once the soul has passed through the various hells and the world of animals and vegetations, and found a place in the world of men, it continues to rise further up till it attains liberation? The Jaina answer to these questions is very simple, and may be given in an English maxim, 'As you sow, so you reap'. Human life is no guarantee for a superior state of consciousness unless it has been worthily lived, and in such a case, there is nothing to prevent its retrogression to subhuman, even to infernal, level. We have seen that even the soul of Mahavira had many progressions and retrogressions before it took the final body. This part of the Jaina view is in perfect conformity with what is contained in the various Upanisads. Read, for instance, the following:

> *Those who possess good conduct here would attain good birth. . . . Those who are of bad conduct here would attain evil birth, the birth of a dog, that of a hog . . .*
> —*Chandogya Upanisad*, V. 10.7

Or,

He is born on this earth as a worm, a grasshopper, a fish,

> *a bird, a lion, a boar, a snake, a tiger, or another creature*
> *in one or other station according to his deeds.*
>
> —*Kausitaki Brahmana*, I, 1.6

There is, therefore, nothing as steady ascent up from human birth which may be taken as automatic. The *Bhagavati Sutra* makes pointed reference to four states of existence and pin-points the sort of activity that may lead to them. They are as follows:

(*i*) Life in hells is the result of possessing immense wealth and indulging in violent deeds.

(*ii*) Life in the subhuman world or the world of vegetation is the result of practising deception and fraud, uttering falsehood, etc.

(*iii*) Life in the world of men is the result of simple behaviour, humility, kindness, compassion, and so on.

(*iv*) Life in heavens is the result of practising austerities, vows and the like.

> —*Bhagavati Sutra*, S. 8, U. 9

Therefore, it is *karma* that decides whither the soul should go. The Jainas believe in the continuity of consciousness throughout the universe, even in things in which others, including modern science, has not yet seen consciousness. All the same, the Jainas, like many others, have conceded a superior status to men because the human body has fitted-in mechanisms which may help him to attain a superior level. But spiritual ascent is no birth right for human beings, nor is it automatic. Neither does human life plug the chances of retrogression down to the lowest level unless it is worthily lived. Rare is a human being who is willing and able to make use of his life for a spiritual end. In this connection, one may recall the worthy parable recorded in the *Uttaradhyayana Sutra* which is as follows:

> *Three merchants move out*
> *With their capital with them*
> *One comes back with profit*
> *Another returns with his capital.*
> *And the third comes back*
> *Even with his capital gone*

Such is parable from business life
In religion, too, it's like this. (VII. 14-15)
By dine of various trainings
Those who become householders devout
Acquiring karma giving human birth
As human beings they are born again.
Those who have vast learning
Add they to their capital
With discipline and special merit
No longer lowly, they attain godhood. (VII. 20-21)
Look at the imprudence of the fools
Who practise unrighteousness
Turning away from what's virtuous
Sinful, they are born in hell.
Look at the patience of the wise
Who fulfil all spiritual laws
Discarding all unrighteousness
Pious souls are born in heaven.
A wise monk contrasts
Foolishness with prudence
He gives up foolishness
And wends through the path of prudence. (VII. 28-30)

Note: The discussion on *jiva* contained in the *Bhagavati Sutra* introduces many items like infernal beings, *karma, lesya, drsti, darsana, jnana, sanjna, sarira, yoga, upayoga,* vices and freedom from them, activities, and so on. The discussion is carried on to a systematic level in the *Prajnapana Sutra* to which Mahavira makes several references in the *Bhagavati Sutra.*

WHILE METAPHYSICS is, in a sense, a scientific enquiry about real or reals, ethics has a goal, a clear purpose, which, in Indian terminology, is the liberation of the soul which is supposed to be in bondage and misery. There are different views of bondage and different ways of attaining liberation of which the Jaina way is one, and is perhaps the most original and significant one.

We have seen in the previous chapter that, with the Jainas, individual soul passes through various existences at the goading of *karma*. For the most part, the soul is a passive agent and hence cannot determine its own course. In this, the Jaina view is not very dissimilar from other views held in India. But a real difference creeps in when the soul is encased in a human body. As an activist, Mahavira has prescribed a conscious effort on the part of the human soul to extricate himself from the clutches of *karma*. As a human being, one has the requisite equipment, consciousness, intellect, perception, etc., fitted into his frame. Besides, he has the facility all around him, so that instead of remaining a tool in the grip of *karma*, he may liberate himself totally from it and build up a rosy future. In other words, the Jainas firmly believe in the English maxim, 'man is the architect of his own future'. This not only makes Jaina ethics an ethics of responsibility, but provides a definite system.

People from God-centred religions have found it difficult to understand the Jaina system, since it contains no God to extend his grace to man. As Sir Charles Eliot (his *Hinduism and Buddhism*, London, 1962, Vol. 1, p. 105) has written: "Many of their doctrines, especially their disregard not only of priests but of God ... seems to us so strange in any system which can be called religion." If men of this line of thinking could be made to replace the notion of 'God' by 'superhuman power' in man, and make man the master of his own destiny, then it may be possible for them to appreciate the beauty and originality of the Jaina system. Mahavira is the

* Dayanand Bhargava's *Jaina Ethics* is a useful work on this subject.

only one among the world teachers who has recognised the immense spiritual possibility in man and inspired him to spiritual action.

In the Jaina view, metaphysics and ethics are the two sides of the same thing. As Samantabhadra has said, without knowing the real nature of things, all moral distinction between the pairs, viz., bondage and liberation, virtue and vice, heaven and hell, pleasure and pain, will be just blurred.

JAINA ETHICS

dhammo mangalamukkittham ahimsa sanjamo tabo

Dharma is the highest weal; it consists of non-violence, self-control and austerities.

The *Dasavaikalika Sutra* open with this significant line.

Ethics, in the western view, is what is right or good in conduct. This should suppose that all is not right or good in conduct. Ethics aims at identifying what is right and good in conduct and suggesting to man to live upto them. For perfection in conduct, the Jainas have a technical word, *samyak caritra*.

We have already seen that in the Jaina view of reality, two principal items are *jiva* and *ajiva*, consciousness and not-consciousness, and in the Jaina view, consciousness is no monopoly of man. This is a very important point. As S. Gopalan has concisely put it,

> ... the Jaina philosophers' referring to the conscious principle has the wholesome effect of making us ponder over the conscious principle in the universe and of making us trace the evolution of consciousness not from the human level alone, but from the very stage of 'its coming into existence'. In this emphasis on taking an integral view of consciousness, we see that far from laying less emphasis on human responsibility, there is a consistent exhortation for man to live really a life worthy of his stage of evolution, first to see that he maintains the level without slipping down, and then to aim at the higher evolution of his consciousness.
>
> —S. Gopalan, *Outlines of Jainism*, pp. 117-18

All life is misery including the life of a human being, and all worldly pleasures are a misery in the end. We have the following instructive lines in the *Uttaradhyayana*,

> *All music is but prattle*
> *All dances no better than mockery*
> *All ornaments are but a burden*
> *All pleasures usher in pains.* 13.16

We have the most charming account of Kapila in Chapter Eight. He came to beg, but turned into a monk. The king wanted to bestow on him one *crora* (10 million) gold coins, but Kapila said, "Sir, I have renounced everything."

So he took nothing and departed. Six months later, he acquired the supreme knowledge, the *kevala jnana*. In the course of his wanderings, he came to a forest outside the city of Rajagraha where lived 500 thieves headed by one Vanabhadra. The thieves caught the monk, and in a light mood, they asked him to dance. When the monk asked who would follow him on the instruments, all of them began to beat their palms. At this, Kapila gave his memorable song whose opening lines were:

> *In this transcient, restless world*
> *Which is full of misery*
> *What acts shall I perform*
> *So that I may not go astray.* (U.S. 8.1)

And the *Uttaradhyayana Sutra* indicates elsewhere,

> *There is a safe place in view of all, but difficult of approach, where there is no old age nor death, no pain nor disease.* (23.81)

The safe place is the abode of the liberated souls. The bondage of the soul starts because of its association with matter, and this association exists from an eternal past. Soul is a self-existent reality as matter is, and the Jainas say that there is no hard opposition between the two as would render them incapable of being united in such a manner as we find in the case of milk and water. For, the attributes of matter are not absolutely contradictory to the attributes of the soul. Matter is not matter in relation to what is not matter, and so is the case with the soul. As a European writer has put it, 'Body and soul are like the peevish man and wife, united, jars, yet loath to part.' The conception of matter is that it has weight and fills up space; but the essence of soul is conceived in self-consciousness absolutely free from any tinge of materiality. But, like the vacuous space, the soul has innumerble space-points which are infinite in number, and these are in occupation by *karma* matter. This is the bondage. The space-points are essentially of the nature of conscious effulgence which seems to have been put out by the superimposition of *karma* matter, like a mirror which becomes covered with dust falling on it and appears non-reflecting in consequence. The goal of ethics is to make the soul clean of the last particle of *karma* matter so that it shines once again and rises to the top of the sphere. There is an infinite number of these souls. And though an infinite number of these have become free from the turmoil of the world, there is still an infinite number scattered all over the universe who are still in bondage. To show them the way to attain liberation is the aim of Jaina ethics.

Dayanand Bhargava gives the following as the salient features of Jaina ethics:

First, it is based on the doctrine of *syadvada* which has saved the Jaina doctrine form being one-sided.

Second, it does not confuse spirituality with social living, and the treatises dealing with the former with liberation as the goal are called the *moksa sastras*, to distinguish them from sociological treatises called *dharmasastra*.

Third, it puts emphasis on the simultaneous fulfilment of code for the sake of acquiring right vision, right knowledge and right conduct.

Fourth, it assigns primary place to the life of a monk which is the first step on the road to liberation. There is a rigorous code even for the followers, but, despite this, they cannot be liberated till they embrace monkhood.

Fifth, it is based on the view of a unity of consciousness so that, basically, all souls are equal.

NINE FUNDAMENTALS

Nine fundamentals in Jainism called *nava-tattva* may be stated in pairs as follows:

jiva-ajiva, punya-papa, asrava-samvara, bandha-nirjara and *moksa* which is a single item. Their nearest English synonyms are soul-non-soul, virtue-vice, *influx of karma* and checking influx, bondage of *karma* and uprooting and throwing them out, and liberation.

Jiva and *ajiva* are the basis reals co-existing in the company of each other. The mere association of soul and matter may not have caused much mischief but for the interpolation of *karma* whose matter particles are in complete occupation of the space-points of the soul. If some portion of *karma* matter is getting out because it has been experienced, fresh *karma* matter is being deposited on the space-points of the soul so that it is at no time free from it. To free the space-points of the soul from the occupation of *karma* matter is the goal of Jaina ethics. It is essentially the ethics of self-realisation in and through self-rule and regulation.

Two parts of Jaina ethics are clear. First, we have to see how the soul, which is in close association with matter, which is bondage, continues to be in this state through time. And second, we have to see the process through which the soul regains its freedom. The process is not automatic, but is the outcome of conscious effort.

If bondage is a phenomenon which has come down from a past period, its perpetuation is the outcome of deeds, both pious and sinful. In the Jaina view, a deed or a thought has any worth only as it is conducive to the realisation of some end to which it is a mean. Thus good thought or deed is conducive to the realisation of something good, as bad thought or deed is conducive to the realisation of something bad. For these two, the Jainas have two words, *punya* and *papa*.

In life, we see that some people living in happiness and some in misery. The people who are happy are so for some good deeds in the past. The people who are miserable are so for some bad deeds in the past. But none of these is ripe for liberation. Liberation stands for escape from the cycle of birth and death and is above virtue and vice, and wholly apart from it.

Virtue gives right vision and right knowledge. Further, it gives pleasant feelings, a good life-span, a good and healthy body and a noble family. The outcome of vice is just the reverse. Though none of these leads to liberation, yet, if one is to choose, virtue is better, since with a reasonable affluence, a good life-span and a good physique, one has greater chances of concentrating on problems of existence and attaining liberation than another who is living his life in adverse circumstances. But a pious life is not an end in itself, nor is it sufficient. The goal is liberation and that must not be lost sight of. The *ajiva* or matter which is in occupation of the soul's space-points has to be thrown out for ever. But, to be able to do so, one has to realise that it is in bondage and that it is being tied by fresh fetters everyday, every moment. So long as this realisation is not there, necessary effort will not follow.

For past fetters, the Jainas have a term, *bandha*, and for the fresh, incoming ones, *asrava*. These two give the process in which the soul is in bondage from the past and is getting entangled afresh everyday. To take up *asrava* first, for such is Jaina chronology, it is the influx of *karma* particles into the soul that perpetuate bondage through time. The requisite powers which galvanise the soul to draw in matter from without are subreption, attachment, passions, oversight and functional activities of mind, speech and body. Affected by these, the soul attracts fresh *karma* matter towards itself. This influx is both subjective and objective. Because of the objective influx, the soul loses resistance to *karma* infection, and because of the subjective influx, it becomes polluted. The process is not dissimilar from what happens when a man falls sick. We are living in a cauldron full of germs. But we do not fall ill every-day because of the resistance of our body. But when, for some reason, this resistance goes, we are sick. The same process operates in the case of *karma* influx. Because of subreption, attachment, etc., the soul loses resistance to *karma* matter and attracts it towards itself and lets it occupy its space-points. And since the process repeats every moment, it becomes almost a habit with the soul.

The other word in the pair, *bandha*, stands for bondage. *Bandha* is interpenetration, as it were, into each other's spheres of soul and *karma* matter making the two appear as one. Like its counterpart, *bandha* is also subjective and objective. The factors causing bondage are the malignant factors of passions and activities of mind, speech and body.

Bandha is considered to be of four kinds, viz., *prakriti-bandha, sthiti bandha, anubhaga bandha* and *pradesa bandha*. *Prakriti bandha* is the result of transformation of matter into *karma* particles due to the vibratory activity of the soul. Thus for all practical purposes, this bondage is due to *karma*. The word *sthiti* in *sthiti bandha* stands for a protentiveness. *Karma* particles which are attracted to the soul and remain there in a relation of total identity with it do not remain so for ever. While some of these particles are always in the process of falling out, others remain there standing in the same relation. Thus two things are involved here. First, there is an incessant flow of karma particles, and second, there is a definite time duration for the defilement to take place.

Anubhaga bandha refers to the intensity of fruition, and follows from *sthiti bandha*. After the *karma* particles have lived their span in the space-points of the soul, they are mature to fructify and cause their experience to the soul. The difference in the intensity of experience, however, depends on the potency of the karma material.

Pradesa in *pradesa bandha* stands for space-points. Once there is the affection of the soul by various types of *karma*, karma particles occupy the space-points of the soul, virtually taking it a prisoner and making it impossible for the soul to escape from the clutches of *karma*. Though fourth in Jaina chronology, *pradesa bandha* should stand second.

If *asrava* and *bandha* stand for the process causing bondage to the soul, the fulfilment of right conduct on the basis of right vision and right knowledge generates two-fold process by which the fresh influx of *karma* particles is stopped, and the particles still in possession of the soul's space-points are simultaneously pulled up at a time through a conscious effort and thrown out wholesale. For these, the technical words are *samvara* and *nirjara*. *Samvara* is thus the process of reversing the flow of *karma* particles which had been defiling the soul. This is also subjective and objective, checking first the susceptibility to receive fresh *karma* matter, which, then, stops the inflow. The susceptibility to receive *karma* particles go as a result of self-apprehension, which means that the soul which has been forgetful of its real nature regains the apprehension that it is consciousness itself.

The instruments for checking the influx of fresh *karma* matter are called *samitis, guptis, yati-dharma, bhavana, parisaha* and *caritra*. *Samiti* refers to carefulness in movement, speech, acceptance of food, etc., so that nothing is perpetrated which is not according to the canonical prescriptions. All these are external activities so that *samitis* take care of external things. Its inner counterpart are the *guptis* which are restraints for controlling inner nature. Their most direct target is the mind which has been considered to be the most wayward of the sense organs. *Yati-dharma*, though primarily intended for a monk, may extend to anyone, and includes items like forgiveness, humility, simplicity, freedom from avarice, austerity, truthfulness, chastity, etc. These are the items which make man perfect, and may find place in any system. *Bhavana* is reflection or thinking within about the real nature and character of origin, use and utility of something. Constant thinking of this sort wakes up the knowledge of the intrinsic value of the object thought upon and helps him avoid such things as would stand in his way of realisation of the object or end he has in view. There are about a dozen types of thinking like thinking about transcience, about the helplessness of the soul in bondage, about the pains and sufferings of mundane life, etc., etc. *Parisahas* stand for hardships without which no one can expect to attain the goal. These hardships make a long list of 22 items like hunger, thirst, cold, heat, insect bite, etc.. Lastly, *caritra* or conduct. Collectively, these items have been called vows (*vratas*) in some texts and penances (*tapah*) in others.

A soul desirous of salvation from the thraldom of senses must make strenous efforts to gradually stop the influx of *karma* matter into the space-points of the soul. The above list indicates the items of vows or penances whose practice is a sure remedy against this influx.

Along with the process of checking influx of *karma* particles into the space-points of the soul, the soul is required to act in such a way as it would be able to throw away the already acquired dirt of *karma* which has been goading it through the cycle of births and deaths. This process is *nirjara*, which, also, is subjective as well as objective.

By hypothesis, the soul in the *nirjara* stage is in possession of discriminative knowledge which brings about a total change in its attitude to suffering, if not in actual suffering, which, however, does not abate till *karma* particles are all swept away. It is this discriminative knowledge that opens the great vista of spiritual possibility for the soul so that it has no more dearth of inspiration to throw out *karma* matter, and be in its original state again. The role of discriminative knowledge is, therefore, important at this stage. Before the soul is in possession of this type of knowledge, it has a sense of attachment to all the pleasant experiences and a sense of distaste and abhorrence to all unpleasant experiences. It forgets that its various experiences are all due to its own previous actions with attachments and abhorrence; and it continues to identify itself with these. This causes a perpetual bondage. With the rise of discriminative knowledge, it becomes clear to the soul that the various experiences, pleasant as well as unpleasant, are not intrinsic to itself, and are but a play of *karma* matter acting and reacting on it. With this realisation, the soul ceases to have attachment to pleasant experiences or abhorrence to unpleasant experiences, and knows to treat them as wholly external, and hence eradicable. At this stage, the soul ceases to be an active participant, and becomes a mere onlooker watching the great drama of the world. By adopting this attitude towards everything that is external to itself, the soul is now fully capable to throw out *karma*.

The last item in the list of fundamentals is *moksa* or liberation. This too is subjective and objective. That modification of the soul which leads to the total annihilation of *karma* is subjective liberation (*bhava-moksa*), and the actual separation of *karma* matter is objective liberation (*dravya moksa*). On the attainment of this stage, the soul is in possession of its innate freedom and can never be bound again. This means that the eternal attraction of the soul for matter and of matter for the soul which brought the two together in an unknown past ceases for the first time, so that matter bids good-bye to the soul and departs for ever. As Umasvati has written, a person attains omniscience when his four terminable *karmas* (*mohaniya, jnanavaraniya, darsanavaraniya* and *antaraya*) are destroyed. After the attainment of omniscience, the causes producing bondage being absent, and *nirjara* near at hand, he becomes free from the four non-terminable *karmas* in due course (i.e. when his body drops). Thus being free from all kinds of *karma*, he attains liberation.

'MOVING AS MOVED'

The *Bhagavati Sutra* opens with a query from Indrabhuti Gautama which is as follows:

> *Verily, bhante, is it proper to call moving as moved, fructifying as fructified, feeling as felt, separating as separated, cutting as cut, piercing as pierced, burning as burnt, dying as dead, and exhausting as exhausted?* To this, Mahavira replied, *Yes, Gautama, it is so; moving is moved, and so on, till exhausting is exhausted.*
> —*Bhagavati Sutra*, S. 1, U. 1

This is a discussion on *karma nirjaras*. Nine verbs have been used in the above quotu. The soul is in bondage with *karma*, and the soul has now the discriminative knowledge and it strives for early liberation. Now, *karma* which comes up in a natural process must of necessity be exhausted by making its consequence felt. But *karma* which is still dormant, and is in occupation of the soul-space must be got rid of through spiritual practices. Through a conscious effort, the living brings up dormant *karma* in order to push it through various stages till exhaustion. The stages are expressed in the form of nine verbs as stated above. Of these, the first four relate to the brininging up of karma from a dormant state, all in very quick succession, to a state where the karma particles have vacated the space-points of the soul, and the last five relate to the stages leading to total exit of *karma* particles. (See Chapter 7 above about the Jamali episode in this connection.)

To be precise, one who is mature for liberation, and has a striving for it, stands virtually on the last stage from which he can liquidate the earlier ones and earn liberation. He brings up *karma* from a dormant state and puts it straight to fructification. At once, the outcome is felt, which is that *karma* matter is speedily separated from the space-points of the soul, which thus stands vacated. By this quick process, he gets rid of *karma* enshrouding faith, vision, knowledge and power. But he has yet to get rid of the remaining *karma* which give name, lineage, life-span and experiences. They go at death. Some of the above verbs have been later explained in the *Sutra* as follows:

cutting of *karma* means transforming *karma* with a long span into *karma* having a short span;
piercing means changing the deep-effect *karma* into a slow-effect *karma* and *vice versa;*
burning signifies the process by which *karma* particles are turned into ordinary atoms of matter so that they are no longer in occupation of the space-points of the soul;
dying signifies the termination of *karma* determining name, lineage, life-span and experiences; and exhaustion means total elimination of *karma* bondage, and hence of suffering. At this point, the soul is free, and restored to its liberation, enlightenment and perfection.

The use of the present perfect tense to signify what appears to be present continuous is justified by Mahavira on the ground that once the goal is set and the process of liberation gets started, it is as good as ended. For, the last thing, which is the goal in this case, is placed first by the striving soul, and then starts the process of liquidation of the intervening stages, so that, once the process is set going, it must reach its end. Hence moving is moved, and so on.

STAGES OF ASCENT

Ethics is not merely a scholastic exercise. It is a means to an end. The end is the attainment of perfection at the termination of misery. But the perfection is not attained by a long jump, and the soul has to pass through various stages of progress up. These stages have been called *gunasthanas*. The word has two syllables, *guna* and *sthana*. In the words of a commentator, the word *guna* stands for the knowledge, vision and faith of the soul in so far as they are inherent in it. From this, some people have translated *gunasthanas* as 'states of virtue', a term which is acceptable if it is not used in a very restricted sense to signify exercises in character-building. The concept is strictly spiritual and covers from the lowest stage of impulsive life in which man is no better than an animal to the highest stage of perfection. The concept of *gunasthanas* is, so to say, a barometer for measuring the stage of spiritual ascent for the soul. It is difficult to get such an elaborate measure in any other system. Although in some of the older texts, only 12 *gunasthanas* have been identified, the list, as it has come down to us has 14 items which are as follows:

1. Wrong believer (*mithyadrsti*)—This is the base at which stands everybody. The soul at this stage is characterised by a spiritual blindness.
2. One with a slight taste of right belief (*sasvadana samyagdrsti*). This stage is normally considered not as an evolution from the first stage but as a result of a fall from a higher stage. One who has slipped down to this stage has to start his ascent again.
3. One with a mixed belief (*misradrsti*). This refers to a state of oscillation where the soul is wavering between wrong outlook and right outlook without attaining the latter. Hence the outlook here is mixed.

4. One with right outlook but not yet disciplined (*avirata samyag-drsti*). With the attainment of right outlook, this stage acquires great importance, though as yet the soul is not yet restrained.

5. One who has partial self-restraint (*desavirata*).

6. One who has full self-restraint though one is not steadfast in it (*pramatta samyata*).

7. One who has full self-restraint and who is steadfast. (*apramatta samyata*).

These three together stand for a struggle in the soul to get rid of partial restraint and be fully lodged in self-restraint. In a sense, they may be taken to be the three phases of the same stage, and are put through within a short span of time.

8. This stage called *nivrtti badara samparaya* is an important stage in so far as in this stage, the soul acquires a rare psychical force which it can use in the subjugation and eradication of *karma*. The soul at this stage has attained a purity which makes it capable to shorten the duration and weaken the intensity of *karma*. Though the influx of fresh *karma* has not yet stopped, but their duration and intensity definitely become less, and the soul has now a confidence in its own capability about dealing with *karma* which becomes an important psychological asset to it.

9. This stage is called *anivrtti badara samparaya*.

10. This stage called *suksma samparaya*. These two together represent a stage where the soul takes new weapons in its armoury in its spiritual ascent. In the ninth stage, the soul gets over gross emotions and crude impulses, and in the tenth stage, it overpowers subtle emotions and passions.

11. This is called *upasanta kasaya vitaraga chadmasta*. At this stage, the passions are set at rest; all attachments are overpowered. But he is still a *chadmasta*, i.e., one who is liable to err.

12. This is called *ksina kasaya vitaraga chadamasts*. While in the previous stage, passions are only set at rest, at this stage, they stand virtually thinned.

13. This is called *sayogi kevali*. This is the stage where the soul attains the supreme knowledge and four of his terminable *karmas* terminate. But since the soul is still encased in a body, with a name, etc., though virtually liberated, it discharges some inescapable activities that go with body and mind.

14. This is called *ayogi kevali*. Here all activities end and the soul enters into complete perfection, enlightenment and liberation.

It will thus be seen that the doctrine of *gunasthanas* is the most logical outcome of Jaina philosophy and ethics. The story is one of steady progress up. By the fourth stage, the wrong outlook goes so that the soul is fit for *samyak darsana*. This makes the soul to acquire right knowledge. And if right knowledge is incorporated in life through right conduct, the soul continues to rise further up towards perfection. But still it is liable to err. From the sixth to the tenth stage, passions and activities exercise their influence. From the eleventh till the thirteenth stage, only activity is present. At the last atage, even activities cease, and hence there is no more binding of *karma*.

IS THE SYSTEM UNSYSTEMATIC

Such is the Jaina system. The goal is perfection for the soul where there is no more bondage of *karma*, and the soul is shining in its pristine purity. We may now note the system, in brief, in a tabular form:

		jiva + *ajiva*	
		(soul) (matter)	
		punya-papa	
		(virtue & vice)	
I.	In bondage	*bandha* (bondage) *asrava* (influx)	
II.	On the road to liberation	*samvara* (checking influx)	*nirjara* (uprooting *karma*)
III.		*moksa* (liberation)	

At the third stage, which is the goal of Jainism, the position is, to use the Buddhist terminology,

sabbam dukkham nijjhinnam bhavissati.

Note: The terms representing the main system and the terms forming corollaries to them are indiscriminately set out together with other terms of a similar import in a passage in the *Sutrakritanga* (II. 5) presenting certain important articles of faith.

PART FOUR

RELIGION

With us, philosophy remains always something collateral only; our mainstay is formed by religion and ethics. But with the Indians, philosophy is life in full earnest; it is but another name for religion, while morality has a place assigned to it as an essential preliminary to all philosophy.   —*Max Muller*

CORE TO Jainism is the doctrine of *karma*, which, as the principle
of causation, occupies a position which is not dissimilar from that
of God in other systems. *Karma* is not merely a subjective principle,
nor a distant abstraction; it has its material content which gets
deposited on the spacepoints of the soul and drags it through space
and time.

The association of soul and matter, spirit and body, is the outcome of *karma* which is itself a body that never goes even at death,
but continues to haunt the soul. The two are so mixed up as if
they are one, and there are systems in which the body has been
confused with the soul. It is *karma* that puts the soul in a suitable
body, it tends to move its limbs and act. Activity may be pious
or sinful, but both create fresh fetters. The Jaina word for activity
is *kriya* or *yoga*, not *karma* as in Buddhism. In Jainism, *karma*
is the cause and the leadingmost cause determining the course of
the soul. It is, therefore, necessary to give an outline of *karma*
theory.

In the canonical texts, karma theory is very old, but the theory
in its current form is a considerable modification on the classical
position, which was comparatively simple. The old doctrine considered the eight chief types without bothering about the subtypes.
The *Bhagavati* contains passages which read like a transition from the
simple, old *karma* doctrine to a more complex one expressed in
terms of the stages of spiritual ascent; but as yet this part was not
adequately developed. The *Prajnapana* confines itself to the eight chief
types of *karma*, the *Avasyaka-niryukti* contains an account of *upasa-
masreni* and *ksapaka-sreni* and the *Tattvartha* refers to them. The
most advanced view about *karma* in the classical texts is, however,
contained in *Sat-khandagama*. But even this would appear to be
relatively simple when compared with the accounts given in *Dhavala*
and *Jayadhavala* by Virasena. In recent years, Acarya Vijaya
Premasurisvara has done comprehensive work on *karma* theory

---

* Helmuth von Glasenapp's *The Doctrine of Karma* is an autho-
ritative text in English which is scruplously honest to the source
material.

in about four *lakh* verses in Sanskrit. (Vide *Jain Journal*, January, 1969).

The *Bhagavati Sutra* employs expressions like *vairena sprista* and *kriyaya sprista* to describe the net result of some wrong done by one to someone else. The *Bhagavati* leaves no doubt that the soul of a person committing a wrong act is permeated by the corresponding *karma*. There are also passages describing in great details the qualifications of one who is going to attain, first, omniscience, and, next, liberation, which might have been the parent of the later-day disussion on the qualifications of a *ksapakasreni-arohi* (wholly liberated being). An interesting item noted in the *Bhagavati* is *kanksamohaniya* which does not figure in later-day discussions. In all probability, this was another word for what has been called *darsana mohaniya*.

In giving reply to a question by Indrabhuti Gautama, Mahavira said,

> It is karma that generates bondage, which means that a living being who has acquired karma is in bondage. Karma is with the soul from an infinite past, and hence the soul is the acquirer of karma from an infinite past period. Of course, not same karma remains affixed for all times; but as fresh karma is acquired in a non-ending series to take the place of karma which wears out through suffering, the soul is in perpetual bondage. A karma flows in, as a karma flows out, then follows the next, and still next, and so on, like the incessant flow of a stream.
>
> —*Prajnapana Sutra*

KARMA AS CAUSATION

Although the chief attribute of the soul is consciousness, not many souls will be found to appear or behave in their own form. The vast majority of them have only a restricted vision, knowledge and energy, adhere to wrong metaphysical doctrines, neglect the code of ethics, experience pleasure and pain, possess manifold individual qualities and have only a temporal limited existence. They are so because they are subject to external influences, for which they look entirely different from what they are. This external influence is that of *karma*.

Karma in Jainism does not mean 'deed' or 'act', nor is it an invisible force like fate or destiny. It is a complex of very fine matter, imperceptible to the senses, which enters into the soul and causes great changes in it. Thus *karma* is something material which produces certain conditions in the soul in the same manner as a medical pill does to the body when it is introduced into the body. The fine matter which may become *karma* fills the entire cosmos. This is called *karman* matter. When the matter of the *karman* variety sticks to the soul, it become *karma*, the soul's destiny, so to say. *Karma* particles settled on the soul's space remain there. When some of these become ripe for fructification, they come up and cause experiences to the soul. The duration and intensity of the effect of *karma* depends upon the state of mind (*adhyavasaya*) of the soul at the time of acquisition. When its efficacy expires, it is dead.

The association of the soul with matter has continued over an infinite past period, but the matter particles are ever changing, and the relation is to last for an infinite period in the future, unless terminated by a conscious effort. Through a series of special processes, the soul may hinder the absorption of fresh *karma* and annihilate *karma* which still lies dormant on the soul's space. If the soul is capable of that, it becomes its own master again, and terminates its slavery to *karma*. Many souls have been liberated in the past from their bondage with *karma* and many will be liberated in future; but still there will be many more tied to the wheels of *karma* and this bondage is, therefore, eternal. The *karma* doctrine has been formulated by the Jainas into a remarkable system with its minute details.

KARMA DIVISIONS

There are many divisions of *karma* as *pradesa karma* and *anubhaga karma*, *ghati karma* and *aghati karma*, *evambhuta* and *anevambhuta karma*, and so on. But the division most popularly known is that between *ghati* and *aghati*, each having four types. *Ghati karmas* are those which an encased soul can terminate while still in body; but *aghati karmas* terminate only when the soul is permanently separated from the body. Four *ghati karmas* are:

1. *karma* enshrouding knowledge (*jnanavarana*)
2. *karma* enshrouding vision/faith (*darsanavarana*)

3. *karma* producing feeling of pleasure and pain (*vedaniya*)
4. *karma* generating delusion (*mohaniya*)

Four *aghati karmas* are:

5. *karma* determining life-span (*ayus*)
6. *karma* giving a name (*nama*)
7. *karma* giving family line (*gotra*)
8. *karma* which hinders the soul in its capability of resolution and enjoyment (*antaraya*).

These eight are the fundamental species (*mula-prakritis*) and each one of the principal *karma* has many sub-species (*uttara-prakritis*).

Of special interest for our purpose is the fourth variety called *mohaniya* which generates delusion. It overpowers both vision/ faith (*darsana*) and conduct (*caritra*). *Darsana-varana karma* is, however, to be distinguished from *darsana mohaniya* in so far as the former enshrouds vision making it virtually ineffective while the latter causes delusion giving a distorted vision as distinguished from the right one. Coming to *caritra mohaniya*, it disturbs right conduct possessed innately by the soul. Thus it hinders the soul from acting according to the religious prescriptions. This disturbance in conduct is produced by the various passions. mini-passions and sex.

Passions (*kasayas*) are four in number called anger, pride, attachment and greed, and each has four sub-species. The degrees of strength of the passions are illustrated by examples. The four species of anger are likened unto a line drawn in stone, in earth, in dust and in water. The first one can be removed only with the greatest difficulty, and then the extent of effort diminishes from one to the other, till at last a line drawn in water needs hardly any effort to make it disappear. In the same manner, anger that endures through life can be combatted with the greatest difficulty, and then the effort needed to wipe out the remaining three varieties of anger steadily diminishes. Likewise, the degrees of pride are to be compared unto a pillar of stone, a bone, a log and the liana of a *dalbergia ougeinensis*, the inflexibility diminishing from one to the next one, till at the last item, the inflexibility is no more than negligible. The sub-species of deceit are to be compared to a bamboo root, the horn of a ram, the urine of a cow and a piece of wood. The degrees of greed correspond to scarlet colour, to great dirt, to small dirt and to a dot of termaric. The scarlet is hardly removable; the great dirt is removable with difficulty; the small dirt does not need much effort to remove, and the easiest to wipe out is a dot of termaric.

The six mini-passions (*no-kasayas*) are laughter, prejudicial liking, similar disliking, sorrow, fear and disgust. All of them cause delusion of conduct so that it becomes difficult for the soul to attain right conduct. The mere sensation of pleasure and pain does not have this retarding effect. This is the reason why the distinction between *vedaniya karma* and *no-kasayas* becomes relevant and important.

Sex passions hinder the soul from obeying the code of conduct and from practising self-discipline. It is of three types, viz., male sex, female sex and eunuch, and their corresponding passions. A man covets the company of a woman, but a man's passion is like straw fire which blazes up and is soon extinguished. The passion of a woman is like fire in a cow-dung hill. A cowdung hill glimmers so long as it is coated with ashes, but the fire bursts out into flames when the hill is poked. The desire in a woman for the company of a man is weak so long as it is not touched, but it grows immensely once she is touched. The sexual desire in a eunuch is exceedingly great, because he does not have the usual sex organs with which to enjoy. His desire is directed to both men and women. Like a fire that burns a township, the sexual desire of a eunuch lasts long and yet derives no satisfaction.

SUNDRY CONSIDERATIONS

The Jaina texts have named four types of existences (viz., celestial, subhuman, human and infernal) and five classes of beings (starting with one sense organ till five) which are the outcome of *jati-nama-karma*.

Five types of bodies have been distinguished as gross (*audarika*), fluid (*vaikriya*), assimilative (*aharaka*), caloric (*taijasa*) and *karman* which are the outcome of *nama-karma*. Of the five body-types, each succeeding one is finer than the one just preceding so that the *karman* body is the finest of all. But the finer a body, the larger the number of matter particles contained in it. Every worldly being is always connected with the caloric and the *karman* bodies, but can, in addition, still possess one or two other bodies. It will thus be seen that the entire universe of living beings is a play-ground of *karma*.

Of the five body-types, *karman* body stands fifth so that it is the finest. It is this body that is the receptacle for *karman* matter. The *karman* body changes every moment because new *karma* is continually assimilated by the soul as some of the existing ones are dropping out. Accompanied by the *karman* body, the soul, at death, discards its other bodies, and betakes itself to the place of its new birth where the *karman* body provides the nucleus round which other bodies come up.

The Jaina texts provide an exhaustive account of the duration of *karma* with minima and maxima given for all conceivable situations. This tenure depends on two factors, viz., the state of mind (*adhyavasaya*) and the strength of the passions (*kasayas*). The more sinful a being is, the longer will be the duration of *karma*; the purer a being is, the shorter is the duration. For the infernal beings, long duration is considered as bad and short duration as good. In higher existences, the sinful is binding a smaller *karma* duration and the pure a longer *karma* duration.

Coming next to the intensity of *karma* (called *rasa* or *anubhaga*), this varies according to circumstances. It corresponds to the compactness of *karma* matter which, in turn, depends on the weakness or strength of the passions.

Since *karma* has an eternal relation with the soul, it is necessary to observe, in brief, the states produced in the soul by *karma*. Five such states are:

(*i*) the essential state (*parinamika bhava*) consisting of the innate qualities of the soul which are not changed through the impact of *karma*;

(*ii*) the state which is the consequence of the unhindered operation of *karma* (*audayika bhava*) consisting of all superimposed attributes of the soul which are the outcome of the fructification of some *karma*;

(*iii*) the state produced by the suppression of *karma* (*aupasamika bhava*) consisting of all states of the soul which become apparent when *karma* generating delusion is suppressed by perfect self control;

(*iv*) the state resulting from the exhaustion of *karma* (*ksayika*

bhava) consisting of all that manifest when *karma* bondage
is totally eradicated; and

(*v*) the mixed state (*misra* or *ksayopasamika bhava*). Here
in this state, the existence of *karma* is still felt, though it
does not fructify. It is inferior to item (*iii*), since, in this
state, karma still lingers. This classification of the states
produced in the soul by *karma* is important because it
helps to define exactly which states of the soul are the
consequences of its own being, which are added through
the fructification of *karma* and which are the outcome of
its annihilation.

The causes for which the soul is in bondage with *karma* and by
which it renews this bondage, and the means to salvation have been
noticed in Chapter 16 as *asrava*, *bandha*, *samvara* and *nirjara* and
their detailed consideration will follow in Chapters 18 and 19. We
should note here the capability of salvation of the entire body of
souls. On this, we have a significant line uttered by Mahavira in
reply to a question by Indrabhuti Gautama which states:

savvatthova jiva acarima anantaguna

(Smallest in number are the *siddhas* or perfected souls and also the
not-to-be-perfected beings called *acarima* or *abhavya*; but infinite
times more than these are the would-be-perfected beings called
carima or *bhavya*).

—*Bhagavati Sutra*, S. 6, U. 3

The terse statement needs explanation. *Siddhas* are those who
have been already perfected and liberated. Leaving aside this group,
there exist some souls which are incapable of being perfected, and
they are to be found in all classes of beings. They are never above
the first *gunasthana* which is wrong faith (*mithyatva*). They feel
themselves quite well in the embodied state, because they do not
know anything better. The would-be perfected souls (*bhavya*),
on the contrary, finally become tired of the wandering in ever new
forms of existence. They acquire right religion, practise self-control
and asceticism, and, in the end, after the lapse of a period of time,
short or long, they attain salvation.

KRIYAVADA

The Jainas thus believe in the possibility of liberation for the largest number of souls. But this liberation does not come as a result of grace from above. It is the outcome of conscious effort on the part of the soul itself, since the misery of the soul has been created by the soul itself, and has not been provided by any external agency. The exact technicality through which salvation is attained will be considered in Chapters 18 and 19. In this section, we notice the basic theoretical support for those spiritual strivings which go by the name of *kriyavada* or doctrine of action. Mahavira is the creator of this technique of *kriyavada* which he himself practised and made his monks to do the same and attain liberation.

The logic of *kriyavada* is very simple. While the soul has been recognised as the conscious principle, the most effective principle is *karma* before which even the soul is helpless. To attain liberation, the effective principle is to be completely counteracted by spiritual action which is within the capability of the (human) soul. Only when the soul exerts itself, it can overpower and overthrow *karma*. The action must be initiated by the soul itself, and none else.

To differentiate Mahavira's *kriyavada* from the heterodox opinions, the Jaina texts, notably the *Sutrakritanga*, have discussed at length the latter opinions collectively called *akriyavada* or doctrine of non-action or passivity. Some of the theories of *akriyavada* as discussed in the *Sutrakritanga* are as follows:

1. There are five gross elements: earth, water, fire, wind and air. From them arise an intelligent principle called the soul. On the dissolution of the five elements, even the intelligent principle ceases to exist. Everybody, prudent as well as foolish, has an individual soul. The soul exists as long as the body exists; but after death, it is no more.
   There is neither virtue nor vice, and there is no world hereafter. On the dissolution of the body, the individual ceases to be.
   There are individual souls. They experience pleasure and pain, and, at death, they lose their state of life.
2. When a man acts or causes another to act, it is not his soul which acts or causes to act. (Identified as the Sankhya school).

3. There are five substances, and the soul is a sixth substance. These six substances are imperishable and eternal by their very nature.

4. Pleasure, pain and final beatitude are not caused by the souls themselves, nor by others, but the individual souls experience them. Such is the lot assigned to them by destiny. Some beings have motion, others not. It depends on certain conditions whether they depend on one state or the other. (Identified as the Fatalists).

5. The world has been created and governed by gods. Some others say that it is created by the Brahman. He created the primeval egg out of which all things have come. Some say that it is produced from chaos.

6. The world is boundless and eternal. It exists from eternity and does not perish. Some others say that it is limited but eternal. The knowledge of the highest being is unlimited. The world is limited in every way.

7. Just as the earth, though it is but one pile, presents many forms, so the self, the *atman*, appears under various forms as the universe.

—*Sutrakritanga* in Jacobi's translation,
Sacred Books of the East, Vol. XLV, pp. 235-39

These diverse views are reduced to just five which are,

1. *Ucchedavada* of Ajita Kesakambala,
2. *Akriyavada* of Purana Kasyapa,
3. *Niyativada* of Makkhali Gosala,
4. *Anyonyavada* of Prakrudha Katyayana, and
5. *Viksepavada* of Sanjaya Velatthiputra.

All these are doctrines of non-action or passivity inasmuch as they fail to inspire action or make an individual responsible for his acts. The *Sutrakritanga* enumerates two types of *kriyavada* which, however, fall short of the Jaina standard. They are:

1. According to some, the soul of one who is pure will become free from bad *karma* on reaching beatitude; but in that state, it will again become defiled through pleasant excitement or hate.

According to them, he who has lived on earth as a restrained monk will afterwards become free from *karma*.
As clear water which was free from defilement becomes
again defiled, so will be the soul. (I. 1.3.11-12)

2. If a savage thrusts a spit through the side of a granary,
mistaking it for a man; or through a gourd, mistaking
it for a baby, and roasts it, he will be guilty of murder.

If a savage puts a man on a spit and roasts him, mistaking
him for a fragment of the granary; or a baby, mistaking
him for a gourd, he will not be guilty of murder.

If anybody thrusts a spit through a man or a baby, mistaking him for a fragment of the granary, puts him on
the fire, and roasts him, that will be a meal fit for the
Buddhas to break fast upon. (II. 6.26-28)

The main formula of Mahavira's *kriyavada* has been stated as
follows:

> *sayamkadan ca dukkham nannakadam*

(The painful condition of the self is brought about by one's own
action, it is not brought about by any other cause.)

—*Sutrakritanga*, I. 12.11

The same is brought out in the *Bhagavati Sutra*.

> —*Bhante ! Does the living being experience the fruits
> of self-created karma?*
> —*Goyama ! Some of these he experiences, but others he
> does not.*
> —*Bhante ! You say, 'Some of these he experiences, but
> others he does not'. Why is it so?*
> —*Goyama ! He experiences those that have come up, but
> does not experience those that are still dormant. . . . And,
> in this manner, all the 24 species. (S. 1, U. 2.)*

As the commentator has put it,

> *svayamkritam karma yadatmana pura*
> *falam tadiyam labhate subhasubham*
> *parena dattam yadi labhyate sphutam*
> *sayamkritam karma nirarthakam tada*

(Of karma created by self in the past, effects good and bad are enjoyed by the self. If the self starts suffering for others' deeds, then self-created action loses significance.)

The *Sutrakritanga* elaborates Mahavira's *kriyavada* in the following manner:

> *Individually a man is born, individually he dies, individually he falls from this state of exisence, individually he rises to another. His passions, consciousness, intellect, perceptions, and impressions belong to the individual exclusively. Here, the bonds of relationship are not able to help nor save one.* (II. 1.41)

> *All living beings owe their present form of existence to their own karman; timid, wicked, suffering latent misery, they are about (in the circle of births), subject to birth, old age and death.* (I. 2.3.18)

> *The sinners cannot annihilate their works by new works; the pious annihilate their works by abstention from works; the wise and happy men who got rid of the effects of greed do not commit sins.* (I. 12.15)

> *Some say: pleasant things are produced from pleasant things. They are those who disdain the noble path and the renowned highest good.* (I. 2.4.6)

> *He who intends to kill a living being but does not do it by an act of his body, and he who unknowingly kills one, both are affected by that act through a slight contact with it only, but the demerit in their case is not fully developed.* (I. 1.2.25)

> *He who knows himself and the world; who knows where the creatures go, and whence they will not return; who knows what is eternal and what is transcient; birth and death, and the future existences of men.* (I. 12.20)

> *He who knows the tortures of beings below; who knows the influx of sin and its stoppage; who knows misery and its annihilation,—he is entitled to expound kriyavada.* (I. 12.21)

It will thus be clear that the nine fundamentals of Jaina ethics from *jiva* and *ajiva* till *moksa* were developed from the necessity for a systematic exposition of *kriyavada*, which is, in its essential features, a theory of soul in its relation with *karma*. An allied doctrine is that of the tinges of the soul called *lesyas* which are imparted by the type of *karman* matter acquired by the soul, and the *Uttaradhyayana* (Chapter 34) has a complete account of the *lesyas*. Suffice it to say here that every individual dies in the same *lesya* in which he is born. When his *lesya* ends with his life, then the soul must get a new *lesya*. A wise man should, therefore, know the nature of these *lesyas*. He should avoid the bad ones and obtain the good ones.

ASRAVA AND BANDHA

THE PENETRATION of matter into the soul and its transformation into *karman* proceeds through the activities by the soul. The species of *karman* into which matter can be transformed is, in addition to *yoga*, conditional upon three other causes, of which each, as long as it operates, creates bondage of a certain number of *karmas*. The four causes of bondage are subreption (*mithyatva*), lack of self-discipline (*avirati*), passions (*kasaya*) and activities (*yoga*).

Subreption causes the bondage of infernal life, life as immobile organisms or as animals with one till four organs of senses, undeveloped body, bad figure, etc.

Lack of self-discipline gives unconsciousness, animal and human state, cold lustre, bad gait, low family surroundings, etc.

Passions cause the worst type of bondage drawing in the largest number of *karma* types, translocation of the body, and also of its limbs, and *sata-vedaniya*.

Activities, which are of three types, viz., those of mind, of speech and of body, cause bondage of *sata-vedaniya*.

Exceptions to the operations of the above causes are the *tirthankaras* or especially gifted persons who are rooted in true belief (*samyaktva*).

As already stated, each *karma* can be bound so long as its cause on bondage is in existence; if the cause disappears, the bondage goes. The causes can only be eliminated successively and not out of their order. So long, therefore, as subreption exists, lack of self-discipline, passions and activities are in operation, and all the *karma* types can be bound. If subreption is eliminated, 16 *karma* types caused thereby vanish, and so forth. If the first three causes of bondage, viz., subreption, lack of self-discipline and passions are extinguished, the soul only binds *sata-vedaniya*. This lasts until the soul returns within the power of passions and binds corresponding *karma* types once again, or till the soul completely annihilates activities, and thus altogether puts an end to bondage.

In the following details, we get a glimpse of actions through which the soul produces a *karman:*

Hostility against knowledge and undifferentiated cognition against those who know, and the means of cognition, denial, annihilation, and hindrance of them, disregard of the doctrine and its commandments, rebelliousness and lack of discipline towards teachers and masters, destruction of books, etc.,—such actions are the causes of bondage of *jnanavarana* and *darsanavarana karma.*

Piety, respect for parents and teachers, gentleness, pity, keeping of vows, honourable conduct, overcoming of passions, giving of alms, fidelity in belief are the causes of bondage of *sata-vedaniya karma*; their reversal causes the bondage of *asata-vedaniya karma.*

The teaching of a false religion, the hindrance of the true religion, the blasphemy of the *jinas*, of the saints, of the images of gods, of the community, of the canons, the rape of sacred objects produce *darsanamohaniya karma.*

The actions caused by the outbreak of passions produce the binding of *kasaya-mohaniya karma.* The one whose mind is confused through joking, liking, disliking, sorrow, fear and disgust, binds the *no-kasaya mohaniya karma.* Slight passionate desire, conjugal fidelity, inclination for right conduct cause *pum-bheda karma;* jealousy, pusillanimity, mendacity, great sensuality and adultery cause *stri-bheda karma;* violent love of pleasure, and strong passions directed towards sexual intercourse with men and women cause the binding of *napumsaka-bheda karma.*

One who tortures and kills other beings, who strives in an extra-ordinary manner after possessions, and is governed by life-long passions obtains infernal life or *naraka-ayus.* The deceitful, the fraudulent, who are in possession of the thorns (which according to the *Tattvartha Sutra* are deceit, sexual enjoyment and wrong faith) binds subhuman life or *tiryag-ayus.* The humble, the sincere, whose passion is slight, bind human life or *manusya-ayus.* One who possesses the right belief, but who only partially or not at all practises self-discipline, whose passions are slight, a heretic, who practises foolish asceticism, and unintentionally extinguishes *karma* (*akama nirjara*), by suffering hunger and thirst involuntarily, who is chaste, who endures troubles, who falls from mountain-heights, who perishes in fire and water,—these obtain the life of celestial beings or *deva-ayus.*

Honesty, gentleness, absence of desire and purity cause the bondage of good, and the reverse the bondage of bad, *nama karma.*

Just recognition of excellence of others, modesty, reverence towards teachers and masters, desire to learn and to teach,—these are the causes of the bondage of noble or *uccair karma;* the contrary cause the bondage of ignoble or *nicair karma.*

(Explaining noble *karma,* the *Tattvartha Sutra* states, in part, as follows:

> Perfect belief, possession of veneration, no breach of vows and laws, permanent practice of knowledge and indifference to worldly objects, according to one's power alms and asceticism, assistance to and readiness to serve the community and the monks, love of the *arhats,* masters, wise men and the doctrine, the fulfilment of the *avasyakas* (essentials), the glorification of the way to salvation, attachment to the confessors of the true religion,—these are the causes of *tirthankara nama karma.*
>
> —Jacobi's translation

The hindering of the veneration of the *jina,* the withholding of food, drink, lodging, clothing, the destroying the powers of others with the help of magic spells, altogether the preparation of hindrances of any kind,—these cause the bondage of *antaraya karma.*

SAMVARA AND NIRJARA

The suppression of the inflow of new *karma* is *samvara.* It is attained by 6 means which are:

1. *Guptis* or controls which mean the right regulation of the activities of mind, of speech and of body.
2. *Samitis* or carefulness in walking, speaking, collecting alms, in lifting up and placing down a thing, and in the disposal of live objects, to avoid sins against *dharma,* and to hinder the killing of living beings.
3. *Dharma* or 10 duties of a monk, viz., forbearance, humility, purity, self-abnegation, truthfulness, self-control,

asceticism, abstinence, voluntary poverty, and spiritual obedience.

4. *Bhavana* or 12 reflections, viz., considering the transitoriness of all things, of the helplessness of man, of the mundane life, of the isolation of the soul, of the heterogeneity of soul and body, of the impurity of the body, of the inflow of *karma*, of restricing the influx of *karma* and of effecting its annihilation, of the world, of the scarcity of enlightenment, and of the truth well-proclaimed by religion.

5. *Parisaha* or the patient endurance of 22 hardships. The embodied soul should be indifferent to them. These hardship are due to hunger, thirst, cold, heat, mosquitoes, nudity or poor clothing, discomfort connected with long wandering, women, a vagrant life, uncomfortable place of residence/meditation, uncomfortable bed, abusive words, ill-treatment, cold reception during begging, failure in begging, sickness, pricking of grass blades on which he lies, the dirt of the body, eulogy, conceit of knowledge, despair concerning ignorance, and doubt about the truth of the doctrine. These troubles are the outcome of *jnanavaraniya, darsanavaraniya, mohaniya, antaraya* and *vedaniya karma*.

6. *Caritra* or conduct.

The annihilation of *karma* is called *nirjara*. It is attained by

(*i*) external asceticism, viz., fasting, reduction of food, restriction to certain food, renunciation of delicacies, a lonely resting place and mortification of the flesh;

(*ii*) internal asceticism, viz., penitence, modesty, eagerness to serve, study, renunciation and meditation.

SAMYAK DARSANA

Earlier, in discussing the life of Mahavira, we said that in one of the fables, Mahavira has been described as the merchant selling 'three jewels'. The three jewels are right faith, right knowledge and right conduct. These three do not represent three different paths, as under Hinduism, but are the three facets of the same path. To the three, the *Uttaradhyayana Sutra* adds austerities as a fourth item.

(Vide Chapter 23). In giving details, however, the *Sutra* concentrates on the first three items only.

Of the three, *samyak darsana* or right faith is considered to be the prime cause of *moksa* inasmuch as it paves the way to right knowledge and right conduct. According to the *Yasastilaka*,

> It is the prime cause of salvation, just as the foundation is the mainstay of a palace, good luck that of beauty, life that of bodily enjoyment, royal power that of victory, culture that of nobility and policy that of government.

The *Uttaradhyayana Sutra* envisages that right knowledge remains unattainable in the absence of right belief and right conduct is out of question without right knowledge. (Vide Chapters 28-30). *Samyak darsana* is itself defined as faith in the seven (nine) fundamentals, viz., *jiva, ajiva, (panya, papa,) asrava, bandha, samvara, nirjara* and *moksa*.

Right faith consists in an insight into the meaning of truths as proclaimed and taught, a mental perception of the excellence of the system as propounded, a personal conviction as to the greatness and goodness of the teacher and a ready acceptance of certain articles of faith for one's guidance. Right faith removes all doubt and scepticism from one's mind and helps to establish or re-establish faith. As we have it in the *Uttaradhyayana*,

> By the teaching of true knowledge, by the avoidance of ignorance and delusion, and by the destruction of love and hatred, one arrives at final deliverance which is nothing but bliss. (Chapter 32.2)

It is no ordinary or blind faith but faith that inspires action by opening a new view of life and the possibility of its perfection. Nine kinds of obstruction to right faith are: sleep, activity, very deep sleep, a high degree of activity, a state of deep-rooted greed, cover to the vision of the eye, cover to the vision of the non-eye, cover to *avadhi-darsana* and cover to *kevala-darsana*. (Chapter 33.5-6)

The primacy of right faith has been explained in the following way: There is no right conduct without right faith or righteousness (*samyaktva*), and this must be cultivated for obtaining right faith. Righteousness and conduct originate together, or righteousness precedes conduct. (Chapter 28.29)

Without right faith, there is no right knowledge; without right

knowledge, there is no virtuous conduct; without virtue, there is
no deliverance; and without deliverance, there is no perfection.
(Chapter 28.30)

The excellence of faith depends on the following eight points:

1, that one has no doubt about the truth of the tenets;
2. that one has no preference for heterodox tenets;
3. that one does not doubt its saving qualities;
4. that one is not shaken in right belief;
5. that one praises the pious;
6. that one encourages weak brethren;
7. that one supports and loves the confessors of *dharma*;
8. that one endeavours to exalt this *dharma*.

SAMYAK JNANA AND CARITRA

When one is fixed in an unshakable faith, it is easy for him to acquire
right knowledge. Right knowledge consists of the knowledge about
substances, qualities and modes. (These items have been considered
earlier). Right knowledge as spiritual knowledge enables the individual to appreciate the nature of the soul in its proper perspective,
and this enables him to adopt necessary practical steps leading to
moksa. These practical steps are collectively the basis of right
conduct. (Vide Chapter 19)

The concept of *tri-ratna* clearly lays down that the ethico-
spiritual discipline is integrated and not isolated. Not any one of
them can be pursued meaningfully and effectively without a simultaneous pursuit of the other two. In the case of an individual, the
most ideal thing would be for all the three to come up simultaneously;
but even if that is not possible, conduct must early follow faith and
knowledge. Which one of the three is basic, it is difficult to say;
but on deeper analysis, it would appear that in the absence of right
faith, neither will knowledge go deep, nor will conduct be firm. This
seems to be a highly practical consideration, and no a mere dogma.

POST-SCRIPT

A post-scropit is needed on two items which are:

(1) *samyaktva* and (ii) *upasama sreni* and *ksapaka sreni*.

Samyaktva, as seen above, stands for righteousness and is,
therefore, a part of right conduct. Spiritual development is conditional upon the elimination of *mohaniya karma*. As the fructification

of a *mohaniya karma* causes the bond of a new *karma* of the same kind, the binding of a new *mohaniya karma* cannot be hindered by a mere good state of mind. To achieve this, three processes called *karana* which are psychical processes all of which last for a fraction of a *muhurta* (48 minutes) have been prescribed. These are called *yatha-pravritti karana, apurva karana* and *nivritti karana.* The fulfilment of these three gives what is called *samyaktva.*

In considering *gunasthanas,* we have said that the list of 14 stages in the ascent up must have come pretty early. But refinements were added by later writers. One important outcome of this refinement is the recognition of the two types called *upasama sreni* and *ksapaka sreni.* At the end of the seventh stage, the soul attains either *upasama sreni* or *ksapaka sreni.*

The series (*sreni*) in which the heaped-up species of *mohaniya karma* are suppressed so that they cannot manifest themselves is called *upasama sreni.* The species are not totally eradicated but lie in a latent state and can occasionally break out again. If, however, the suppression takes place in a regular and systematic way, the series may end in a complete suppression of all deluding karma, and the soul reaches the 11th stage. At this stage, the suppressed passions break out again and the soul descends from the 11th stage.

The series called *ksapaka sreni,* in contrast, leads to the destruction of *karma.* The person who has ascended this series annihilates successfully different species of *karma* that lie in a dormant state, and being in the end quite free from *karma,* he achieves the highest goal which is *moksa* or salvation.

Moksa is the state of the released. While eternally ascending and descending periods of time are following one another in constant change, and souls, infinite in number, are continually wandering through the terrific ocean of worldly life, unaffected by the doings of the world, the perfected souls remain in their serene rest, freed from the torments of bodily existence, released from the cycle of births and never returning to it.

> *The orb of day and night, the wandering stars*
> *Again to sight their heavenly courses bend;*
> *The soul, released from the grasp of earthly bars*
> *Soaring in highest space doth ne'er descend.*
> —*Sarva-darsana-samgraha,* p. 33

PRACTICE MAKES perfect,—so goes the proverb. Jainism is a practical religion which is meaningless unless it is made to percolate into one's own life.

Consistent with this, the emphasis of Jainism is on right conduct. Right conduct includes the rules of conduct which have to be observed with meticulous care. These rules not only lay down the way to *samvara* and the way to *nirjara* but also a complete *dharma* which must be fulfilled by a monk (*sramana*) as well as a follower (*sravaka*).

The English word for a *sravaka* is 'follower', though etymologically, the word should mean, 'one who listens'. This makes a *sravaka* more than a follower. Strictly speaking, *sravakahood* is a stage preparatory to monkhood and is compulsory. Therefore, one who does not fulfil the *sagaradharma* or the code for the householder falls from the status of a true follower.

Internally, as well as to the external world, Jainism is better known by the five vows it has prescribed for the monks as well as the lay followers, more particularly *ahimsa* or non-violence. *Ahimsa* is the leader, since in its fulfilment, the other four are fulfilled. They are: non-lie (*amrisa*), non-sex (*amaithuna*), non-theft (*acaurya*) and non-possession (*aparigraha*). These five vows, when applied to the monks are called 'great vows' or *mahavrata*, and when applied to the followers, they are called 'lesser vows' or *anuvrata*. These five vows are so very important that because of them, Jainism is called as the religion of five vows or *pancayama dharma*.

According to the canonical texts, Jainism was the religion of five vows at the time of Rshabha when people were straight and simple. During the period of the remaining 22 *tirthankaras*, when people were simple and wise, the vows were reduced to four. But in view of the arrival of bad times when people had lost their simplicity and had become crafty, Mahavira made it a religion of five vows again and prescribed elaborate rules. The *Acaranga* makes distinct reference to Mahavira's *pancayama*. The interesting thing is that at the time of Mahavira, there lived many monks who belonged to the order of Parsva. Some of these came into contact with

Mahavira or his *ganadharas* and changed over to the religion of five vows.

Jacobi finds evidence of the two forms in a Buddhist text *Samannaphala Sutta*. Writing on the *Sutra*.

caturyama samvara sambhuto

Jacobi maintains:

> It is applied to the doctrine of Mahavira's predecessor, Parsva, to distinguish it from the reformed creed of Mahavira, which is called *pancayama dharma*.
>
> —*Indian Antiquary* IX, p. 160

Elsewhere, in his translation of the *Uttaradhyayana Sutra*, Jabobi writes:

> The argumentation in the text presupposes a decay of the morals of the monastic order to have occured between Parsva and Mahavira. . . .

This interpretation of Jacobi of the significance of the addition of celibacy to the list of vows is now widely accepted. A minority view is, however, that Mahavira added the vow of non-possession, not celibacy.

It is interesting that the vows have been given in negative form as non-possession, etc. The use of the negative prefix has been misunderstood by many western and non-Jaina readers on the ground that these vows do not suggest a positive approach. But those who, like S. C. Thakur (his *Christian and Hindu Ethics*, London, 1969, p. 202), have seen in the negative prefix a positive content have committed no less a mistake. The positive form of non-violence, e.g., is love, kindness or compassion, but these may be virtues, not vows. And as already said, virtues are as much binding as vices, and must be shunned. Therefore, the Jainas wanted non-violence, not love, and so on. And this must be correctly understood.

CONDUCT

In the previous chapter, we saw that in the list of items that check influx of fresh *karma*, the sixth and last item is conduct. Obviously, this means right conduct which includes the following:

1. *samayika* or regular practice to acquire equanimity;

2. *chedopasthapana* or recovery of equanimity after a fall from it;

3. *parihara visuddhika* or purification produced by peculiar austerities;

4. *suksma samparaya* or reduction of desires; and

5. *akasaya yathakhyata* or annihilation of sinfulness according to the precepts given by the *arhats* or *jinas*.

—*Uttaradhyayana Sutra*, Chapter 28

GREAT VOWS

Five great vows which are compulsory for the monks are non-violence, non-lie, non-sex, non-theft and non-property. These are to be practised in their most rigorous form without indulging in relaxation in any way.

The idea of non-violence follows from the Jaina view of life. This view rejects the simple definition of nature as everything minus man, but sees life even in earth, water, air, fire and all forms of vegetation. The soul exists in diverse existences in consequence of its own *karma*, and to disturb it in any way is to create an obstruction in the process of its experiencing the outcome of its own *karma*. Thus understood, non-violence ceases to be a compassion and becomes a right of every soul to experience the outcome of its own *karma* undisturbed. In the words of the *Tattvartha Sutra*, *himsa* is injury or violence caused to the living organism and actuated by passions like pride, prejudice, attachment and hatred. This makes it clear that the physical act is not separated from the mental attitude, and the two are equally important. Co-ordination between mind and body is thus necessary for the practice of non-violence. This should be accompanied by proper and measured speech. In other words, the principle of non-violence implies purity of thought, word and deed.

The second great vow is non-lie. The spirit of the vow is that non-violence being the most important virtue to be followed, every other vow must contribute to strengthen the first one. The best way to practise this vow is to talk little, and if the situation be inconvenient, to leave the place. There are many accounts of Mahavira's life to indicate that he was extremely measured in his speech, and was mostly silent. A man who talks much must inevitably indulge in falsehood.

The vow of non-theft restricts the use of things to what one has so that he does not even pick up a fruit fallen under a tree unless bestowed on him by the master of the tree. Stealing from another generates violent thought and violent action, and is, in consequence the violation of the first great vow. This is not merely a form of ethics, but a part of their religion with the Jainas.

The vow of non-sex in the case of a monk implies a complete abstention from sex in any form. From the accounts available, it should appear that Buddha was totally against taking women in the order as nuns, but had to yield under pressure from his close associates. Mahavira had no such misgiving which, in part, was the outcome of the Jaina tradition which made the order four-fold. But he was not unaware of the difficulty created by the presence of the nuns or *sravikas* in the order, and so he took care of it by prescribing rigorous rules of conduct regarding sex and strictly enforcing them.

The last great vow is non-possession. For a monk, whose possession is reduced to the minimum, non-possession is a part of his life, and in its extreme form, it means nudity, use of the palm as the begging bowl and lying on the bare ground. More important than the physical possession in this case appears to be the mental attitude towards life which needs be based on a total detachment to objects constituting property. Man's attachment towards his home and kith and kin as well as towards so many other things relating to them becomes so much that it will not be an exaggeration to maintain that he considers them all as his 'possession'. The true ascetic has to practise the quality of detachment to such an extent that he will consider everything including his body and mind as hindrances to his reaching the goal of life which is liberation.

Women have been considered to be a chattel from very early times. During the days of 22 *tirthankaras* preceding Mahavira, non-possession of women was a part of this vow, and was not separately emphasized. But, as already seen, Mahavira separated it and named it non-sex.

LESSER VOWS

The great vows become lesser vows called *anuvrata* when they are applied to the lay followers. Laymen cannot observe the vows so strictly as the monks are required to do, and so, consistent with their life as householders, some relaxations are made. But it should be borne in mind that the practice of *anuvratas* is a must for the followers, and one has no right to consider or call himself a *sravaka* unless he practises them.

In the case of non-violence, the householders are permitted to cultivate and to cook without which life becomes impossible. This would involve hurt to one-òrgan beings and is unavoidable. But even this should be reduced to a minimum. But even the householders are required to be very particular in not killing organisms having more than one sense organ.

Similarly about non-lie. The Jaina philosophers were very much alive to the fact that in his everyday life, the householder could not avoid all words that would hurt another, and that would entangle him. Sometimes, and in some situations, uttering falsehood was necessary for his household, profession, even security of his own person. So exceptions were made with regard to these and avoidance of falsehood in regard to all other aspects was all that was advocated as constituting the essence of the lesser vow of non-lie.

The observance of non-theft in the case of the householder meant his not taking things belonging to others, or not taking things which were placed or dropped or forgotten by others. Similarly, the householder was to avoid purchasing things at cheaper prices if the cheaper price was due to an improper method employed in acquiring the object. Underground and unclaimed property belonged to the king, and the householder was required not to take or touch them. If he found any such thing, no matter what its worth, he was required to inform the king about it and surrender it promptly.

The observance of non-sex in the case of the householder meant restricting oneself to the enjoyments with one's married wife, and not to extend it to any other woman. Total non-sex for a householder would be not only ridiculous, but impossible. That would lead to the extinction of the race. The Jaina philosophers were not blind to this aspect. For all practical purposes, therefore, this meant monogamy. Considering the practice of '*niyoga*' which was prevalent in the Indian society which permitted a woman to book a man for her sex pleasure and/or procreation, the Jaina lesser vow of non-sex must be considered to be highly advanced. The practical usefulness of this vow is too apparent for the sake of domestic peace. Even thinking of other women or men would be doing damage to the principle. Leading a strict monogamic life is synonymous with observing sex purity, and it helps the individual to improve the quality of his/her life.

And finally non-possession which in the case of the householder means restricting one's possession, and not wholly getting rid of it. In a sense, this is restricting one's desire for riches and earthly possessions which have caused some of the mightiest upheavals in contemporary history. It is the over-accumulation of wealth which is called its concentration giving rise to gross disparities in society which has given rise to class consciousness in the capitalist societies in the world. At the same time, the fact remains that without certain amount of capital formation, no society or individual can live a progressive economic life. And the Jaina philosophers were not forgetful of this. Besides, lurking behind the lesser vow of non-possession is the need for honesty in trades and professions which is conducive to the greatest good of the society. Trade and industry for a profit motive is a base social ideal. These should not be ends in themselves, but means to a noble end which is to help equitable distribution of national output in which the men of business are mere agents. The ideal is well expressed in the word '*mahajan*' which is a word for the business community in India and which means a 'noble person'. Since the Jainas are the most dominant business community in the country with a large slice of national income in their hands, in the interest of economic stability, the ideal of non-possession holds a great potentiality. In the case of the house-holder, it may not be total *aparigraha* but *parimita parigraha* or limited possession.

The five ethical principles are guides to cleaner life which, next, may turn in search of one's own self. The integrated nature of these ethical principles should be evident from the fact that all of them are ultimately to be measured in terms of non-violence which has been declared by the Jainas to be the highest virtue or *paramo dhamma*. It is the highest not only because all other virtues enter into it as the rivers enter into an ocean, it is also the highest because it leaves the highest principle of nature unmolested when everyone is left free to undergo the experiences with *karma* bondage and build up one's own destiny.

SILAVRATAS

These *vratas* constitute a supplementary list with the lesser vows for the lay followers. They are seven in number as follows:

(*i*)   *digvrata* or taking a lifelong vow to limit his worldly activity to fixed points in all directions;

(*ii*)   *desavrata* or taking a vow to limit the above also for a limited area;

(*iii*)   *anartha-danda-vrata* or taking a vow not to commit purposeless sins;

(*iv*)   *samayika* or taking a vow to devote a particular time (48 minutes for one *samayika*, and like this any number) everyday to reading from sacred texts or contemplation about self;

(*v*)   *pausadha* or taking a vow to live like a monk for a certain period of time;

(*vi*)   *upabhoga-paribhoga-parimana* or taking a vow everyday limiting one's enjoyment of consumable and non-consumable things; and

(*vii*)   *atithi-samvibhaga* or taking a vow to take one's food after feeding some monk, or at least some devoted householder.

Of these seven, the first three are called *gunavratas* or vows multiplying the quality of the five principal vows; and the remaining four are called *siksavratas* or disciplinary vows. The latter are preparatory for the discipline of a monk's life. Thus the five *anuvratas* and seven *silavratas* constitute a bunch of 12 vows which are prescribed for a lay follower.

DASAVAIKALIKA

The *Acarganga* is the oldest existing text on the rules of conduct for the monks. But ever since the production of the text of the *Dasavaikalika Sutra* about 2300 years back, it replaced the *Acaranga* in the curriculum of study by the monks. This, however, does not make the Acaranga obsolete. The author of the *Dasavaikalika Sutra*, Acarya Sayyambhava, was the fifth Head of the order since Mahavira, and, therefore, there is reason to believe that he lived at a time when the tradition created by Mahavira was still fresh. He wrote this thing based on the existing Jaina texts for the use of his son who was destined to have a very short life. The text is important in so far as it lays down not only a complete code of conduct for the monks, but also a complete code for the householders in their relation with the monks so that the former would help the latter in the fulfilment of their vows.

The *Sutra* has ten *Adhyayanas* or Prescriptions. Prescription one states that religion is the highest bliss and is made up of noninjury, self-restraint and penance. Prescription two deals with monkhood which is the first effective step on the road to liberation. This is attained on renunciation of mundane life, followed by faith in, and practice of, restraint which is the central theme of this Prescription.

Prescription three deals with the behaviour or conduct of a monk, and is specific and categorical as to what he is to discard in order to remain fixed in right conduct. A monk who is free from worldly ties is well acquainted with the ways of *karma* influx, is well restrained to all classes of living beings and has a complete command over his sense organs.

Prescription four which deals with non-violence prescribes a thorough examination of the presence of life in various living things of the world. Life exists wherever there is growth with or without movement (since Jaina biology contains elaborate account of forms of life that have no movement). A monk ought to see that no violence of any kind, by mind, speech or body, is done to any living being, howsoever small, insignificant and invisible.

Prescription five deals with selection of right food, including search for it, the mode of acceptance, of bringing and of sharing it with fellow monks. The rules are very detailed and elaborate living no gap at any stage.

Prescription six entitled "On determining Conduct" is a brilliant exposition of *dharma*. A monk should not tell a lie nor indulge in sex behaviour. He should not take anything, howsoever insignificant, without begging. In other words, begging is an important ingradient of mendicancy. He should never injure anyone himself, nor order another to do so, nor approve it in others. He should observe rigorous restraint avoiding four things which are unwholesome for him, viz., food, residence, cloth and bowl. While begging, he is not allowed to sit except under very exceptional circumstances.

Self-introspection and regular confession to a senior monk or *acarya* is a regular part of his life.

Prescription seven deals with the purification of speech. Prescription eight entitled 'Conduct' gives further details on restraint. A monk by definition is one who is endowed with right knowledge and right conduct, and who is fixed in restraint and penance. Prescription nine deals with humility which is considered to be very important for the monk. It is stated that just as the root is the first important thing in the tree which helps to give it trunk, branches, twigs, leaves, flowers, fruits and ultimately juice, so humility is the very root of the monk's conduct whose ultimate juice is liberation. Prescription ten deals with several items of spiritual ecstacy. It is stated that a real monk is he who recognises birth and death to be the real dangers, who exercises control over his limbs and sense organs, who cares not for his own life, and who is always steady and above deceit. He is neither proud of caste nor of form, gain or earning, but is wholly devoted to spiritual meditation.

---

* An English translation of *Dasavaikalika Sutra* with Prakrit text and commentaries by the present writer has been published by Motilal Banarsidass, Delhi, 1973.

THE EVENT took place in Mahavira's life as a monk. Later, he delineated it to his dear disciple Indrabhuti Gautama. It is given below
in his own words:

> *Wandering from place to place and moving from village
> to village I came near a slab of stone under an
> excellent asoka tree in a forest strip named ₁Asoka of the
> city of Sumsumarapura. Having arrived there, beneath
> that excellent asoka tree, on the slab of stone, I courted
> fasts missing six meals at a time, and then having contracted
> both my legs, with hands hanging downward, with my vision
> fixed on a single object, with eyes without a wink, with the
> upper half of the body slightly bent, ane having controlled
> all my sense organs, I courted mahapratima for a night and
> went into meditation.*   —Bhagavati Sutra, S. 3., U. 2

Mahavira is stated to have performed a *pratima* called *sarvatobhadra* in which one performs meditation in the *kayotsarga* posture
for one day-night (24 hours) facing the ten directions. *Kayotsarga* is a posture in which one loses body sense. This is one form.
In another form, *sarvatobhadra* may be 'easy' and 'difficult',
or *laghu* and *maha* as they are called. The *laghu-sarvatobhadra* is
a series of fasts starting with a fast for a day-night missing four meals
till the lighest duration of five day-nights missing 12 meals. It
takes 3 months and 10 days to complete. The fasts can be arranged
as follows:

1	2	3	4	5
3	4	5	1	2
5	1	2	3	4
2	3	4	5	1
4	5	1	2	3

The duration of *maha-sarvatobhadra* is 1 year 1 month and 10
days. In this case, the longest fast is for seven day-nights missing

in all sixteen meals. Apparently, this is more difficult. The fasts can be arranged as follows:

1	2	3	4	5	6	7
4	5	6	7	1	2	3
7	1	2	3	4	5	6
3	4	5	6	7	1	2
6	7	1	2	3	4	5
2	3	4	5	6	7	1
5	6	7	1	2	3	4

Many of Mahavira's monks are stated to have performed the *pratimas.* Thus Skandaka Parivrajaka who later became a monk in Mahavira's order first performed *bhiksu pratima*, and then *guna-ratna-samvatsara.* He first performed the monthly *bhiksu pratima*, then two-monthly, and so on, till seven-monthly *bhiksu pratima*, then the first course of seven day-nights, the second course of seven day-nights, the third course of seven day-nights, a whole day-night, a whole night, in all a course of 12. Then he performed the more difficult one, *guna-ratna-samvatsara.* Practised over a period of 16 months, it entails 407 days of fasting and 73 days of breaking the fast. The fasts can be arranged as follows:

			days of fasting								break	total
			32	16	16						2	34
			30	15	15						2	32
			28	14	14						2	30
			26	13	13						2	28
			24	12	12						2	26
		33	11	11	11						3	36
		30	10	10	10						3	33
		27	9	9	9						3	30
		24	8	8	8						3	27
		21	7	7	7						3	24
	24	6	6	6	6						4	28
	25	5	5	5	5	5					5	30
	24	4	4	4	4	4	4				6	30
24	3	3	3	3	3	3	3	3			8	32
20	2	2	2	2	2	2	2	2	2	10		30
15	1	1	1	1	1	1	1	1	1	1	1 1 1 1 1 15	30

There are many other forms of chain fasts such as *bhadra pratima* which lasts for two days, *mahabhadra pratima* which lasts for four day-nights, *yavamadhya chandra pratima* which lasts for a month, *vajramadhya candra pratima* also lasting for a month, *sapta saptamik pratima* lasting for 49 days, and so on. The physical impact of these penances is undeniable. Severe penances like *gunaratna samvatsara*, make the body unworthy of living any longer, and are courted only when the person concerned is determined to end his life.

There are eleven *pratimas* prescribed for the householders. These form a series of duties and performances which is helpful in creating an attitude resembling monkhood. They rise by degrees and every stage includes all the virtues practised in those preceding. They are:

  (i) *darsana pratima*—possessing complete faith in Jainism (duration one month);

 (ii) *vrata pratima*—fulfilling 12 *vratas* (duration 2 months); at least.

(iii) *samayika pratima*—performing *samayika* at least thrice daily and fulfilling a vow called *desavakasika* (duration 3 months);

 (iv) *pausadha pratima*—living like a monk on certain days of the fortnight (duration 4 months);

  (v) *ratri-bhukta-tyaga pratima* or *kayotsarga pratima* — abstaining from food after sun-set and meditating in *kayotsarga* posture at night (duration 5 months):

 (vi) *brahmacarya pratima*—maintaining sexual purity (duration 6 months);

(vii) *sacitta pratima*—refraining from plucking fruits, etc., and eating uncooked vegetables (duration 7 months);

(viii) *aranbha pratima*—not indulging in any endeavour in mundane affairs (duration 8 months);

 (ix) *presya pratima*—not to order others to endeavour (duration 9 months);

  (x) *uddista-varjana pratima*—retiring from mundane life (duration 10 months); and

11

(xi)   *sramana-bhuta pratima*—living almost like a monk (duration 11 months).

The householders are advised to ascend these steps. Those who have done it are given special importance by the Digmavaras, while the Svetamvaras consider then like ascetics.

PART FIVE

SCIENCE

utpada-drauvya-vyaya
(Genesis-Permanence-Destruction)

—*Bhagavan Mahavira*

IN THAT period, at that time, there was a city named Krtangala. In the outskirts of that city, at a place between the north and the east, there was a *caitya* named Chatrapalasaka. Mahavira was stationed there with his party of monks.

Not far from the city of Krtangala, there was a city named Sravasti. In that city, there lived a great scholar named Skandaka who belonged to the Parivrajaka order.

In the same city, there lived a *Vaisalika-sravaka* who was a great follower of Mahavira. One day, he came to Skandaka and said, "Oh Magadha ! Are the spheres with limit or without limit ? . . ."

But Skandaka had no clear answer. So he remained silent. Meanwhile, he came to know that Mahavira was stationed at a nearby place. So he decided to go to him and put the same questions to him, and get his views. No sooner did he think like that than he started. Mahavira saw him coming and realised his purpose.

In giving his answer to the questions, Mahavira said, in part, as follows:

> The spheres have to be viewed from four angles, viz., as substance, as place, as time and as phenomena.
> As substance, the spheres are one and with limit.
> As to place, the spheres are said to be extended over innumerable crores of yojanas in length and breadth, and over innumerable crores of yojanas in circumference, but still with limit.
> As to time, the spheres existed in the past, they exist in the present and they will exist in the future. There was, there is and there will be no time when there were no spheres. The spheres did exist and will continue to exist. The spheres are fixed, eternal, permanent, non-depreciating, non-wearing out, ever-existent and without limit.
> As phenomena, the spheres are with limitless colours, smells, substances and touches, with limitless physical structures, with limitless heaviness and lightness, with limitless non-heaviness non-lightness, and without limit.

165

> *So, you see, Skandaka, as to substance, the spheres are*
> *with limit, and so are they as to place; but as to time, the*
> *spheres are without limit, and so also without limit are*
> *they as phenomena.*   —*Bhagavati Sutra*, S. 2, U. 1

The *Bhagavati* has innumerable reference to cosmos. In later period, scholars have worked extensively in this field. Among the Jaina scholars, perhaps the most outstanding was Yati Brsabha (A.D. 473-606) who produced the celebrated *Tiloya Pannatti*, and in the western world, perhaps, Kirfel's *Die Kosmogarphie der Inder* was the most systematic exposition on this subject. Yati Brsabha apart, among other works on cosmography, deserving mention are *Samayasara*, *Pancastikaya* and *Pravacanasara* by Bhagavat Kunda-kundacarya (1st century Vikrama), *Mulacara* by Bhattakeracarya, *Harivamsa Purana* by Jinasena Suri (840 Vikrama), *Trilokasara* by Nemicandra Siddhanta Cakravarty, *Jambu-dvipa Pannattii*, *Bhagavati Aradhana*, *Loka Vibhaga*, etc.

Human mind has been attracted to an understanding of cosmos from very early times. This explains why it existed in Babylon, in Greece and in ancient India. For the Jainas, however, a study of cosmos is of special significance, since it demonstrates on a map how a living being inhabiting the central part of the sphere as an animal or a human being may go up to heaven by pious deeds or may rot in one of the hells because of sinful activities. This is an effective way of fixing a man on the right path. But, more than this, *moksa* in the Jaina view does not envisage an imaginary Absolute, but points to a place at the crest of the spheres where a soul perfected, enlightened and liberated, repairs after discarding this body. Thus liberation becomes a spatial concept with the Jainas where the soul which is moving back and forth within a certain portion of the spheres attains to the topmost spatial position. This would have been impossible but for a systematic study of the cosmos.

The salient points of the Jaina stand may be noted in brief. In the first place, the Jainas do not interpolate God into their theory in any form. Second, according to the Jainas, both *loka* (spheres) and *aloka* (sky beyond the spheres) are timeless and have always been in existence. Third, according to the Jaina view, both *jiva* and *ajiva* (soul and matter) are innumerable and timeless; they have always been in existence and will remain so without losing intrinsic property. This agrees with the scientific view only in part, viz., that the presence of matter has to be assumed as stated before, but in the scientific view, *jiva* or organism is not eternal, but came into existence much later when environment became congenial for its existence. The Jainas believe that the *jivas* are not only infinite in number, but are also timeless like matter. The Jainas do not believe in Darwin's theory of gradual evolution of a lower organism into a higher one over time, but believes in the progress or otherwise in the soul which is recorded in the state of existence to which it is assigned because of its *karma*. Thus the Jaina view clashes with Darwinism not on similar ground on which the Christian theology clashes with it, but on a scientific ground of its own. A fourth point made by the Jainas is the emphasis on Genesis-permanence-destruction (*utpada-drauvya-vyaya*) which mean that things are born or take form, they die or undergo transformation, and still there is an element of permanence in them because of which they do not lose their identity, but remain identifiable for all times. It is of interest to compare this with the Steady-State theory according to which the age of the universe is infinite (an element of 'permanence'), but the age of each bit of matter in the universe is finite (i.e., liable to 'genesis' and 'permanence' in the Jaina terminology), since matter is assumed to spring into being uniformly throughout space at just that rate necessary to replace the continuing loss of nebulae over the observers' horizon.

JAINA VIEW OF COSMOS

In the Jaina view, there is but one *loka* (spheres) and one *aloka* (sky), the latter surrounding the former on all sides like a hollow sphere but being out of reach because, beyond the boundary of the spheres, the media of motion and rest cease to exist. Viewed in its vertical cross section, the *loka* narrows from below to the centre, and above the centre, it widens again, almost to the same extent as just below, and then its width diminishes, till at the top, its surface becomes flat. It has thus three parts, upper, central and lower, with widely differing denigens therein. As to the overall look of the *loka*, however, models vary. One model has compared the lower, the central and the upper parts respectively with a bed (*paliyanka*), a thunder-bolt (*varavaira*) and a musical drum turned upside (*uddha mranga*). In another model, the lower and central sections are likened to a conch (*tappa*) and to a cymbal (*jhallari*), and in still another, the whole *loka* is compared with a broad-bottomed vessel (*supaitthaga*). In all these models, the horizontal cross-section is indicated to be circular. A Svetamvara source, *Lokaprakasa*, imagines the *loka* as three pyramids one upon the other, each having a square base and rising in steps on all sides, the central pyramid standing on its top surface. In contrast, the description given by the Digamvaras show three roof-like bodies of the same length but of a steadily diminishing width. Different measures are given of different sections, and these, in fact, dominate in the non-canonical texts. According to one non-canonical conception, the *loka* looks like a *loka-purusa*, i.e., it has the appearance of a human male.

The Jaina models of the ordered system of cosmos contain detailed accounts about the 24 species of their denigens, many in the words of Mahavira himself in reply to Indrabhuti Gautama. Of these, most dominant is the account of the infernal beings. These accounts are not only detailed but also systematic, starting with the inhabitants of the hells beneath, followed by those pertaining to the demigods at the uppermost part of the lower sphere, followed by the prestages of the animals, their lower species, followed by higher and more developed animals, reaching ultimately to human beings, and then to gods of diverse status depending on their spiritual attainments residing at different levels of the upper sphere, rising ultimately to the abode of the liberated souls called Siddhasila. With this, the *loka* comes to an end.

It will be of interest to interpolate here the stand taken on loka and aloka in the *Bhagavati Sutra*. In a characteristic fashion, the text repeatedly refers to the authority of Parsva—*pasena arahaya purisadanienam sasae loe buie* (Arhat Parsva, the leader of men, has called the *loka* eternal). This definitely makes the Jaina theory of cosmos older than Mahavira who was following the tradition. In explaining his views or driving home a point, the illustrations made use of by Mahavira indicates how, in the absence of a lab, complicated concepts can be presented in the form of most common-place illustrations. Thus we are told that the *loka* lies in the midst of *aloka* just as an island lies in the midst of an ocean, a ship lies in the midst of waters, a hole lies in the midst of a piece of cloth, shadow lies in the midst of sun-shine. Similarly, we are told by Mahavira in conversation with a monk that *loka* and *aloka* are coeternal in the same manner as a hen and an egg are, inasmuch as an egg cannot come into existence without a hen, nor a hen without an egg. Two analogies of a leather bag are employed by Mahavira to justify the Jaina belief that the earth rests on water, water on air, air on sky. Finally, we have taken note of the dialogue where it has been argued that a god standing at the far end of the *loka* cannot move about his limbs inside *aloka* because the latter has no motion and rest.

The discussion on cosmos is carried on a high level in the *Prajnapana Sutra* wherein more technical points are taken up for consideration. Chapter Fifteen on 'Organs of Senses' (*Indriyapada*) raises the question whether *loka* is or is not touched by *dharma*, a part of *dharma*, units of *dharma*, by *adharma*, a part of *adharma*, units of *adharma*, by *akasa*, a part of *akasa*, units of *akasa*, by static beings, by mobile beings, by *addhasamaya*. And the question is repeated about *aloka*, about Jambudvipa and the remaining isles (continents). Chapter ten entitled *Caramapada* raises a point about a border region and an intermediate region between loka and aloka which, in the light of contemporary theories of cosmology and cosmogony, may be anybody's guess as to what these regions are. Here it is supposed that the *loka* and *aloka* are made up of a border region and an intermediate region, and the question is raised about the relative numerical strength of the substances, those lying within its intermediate region, those lying within the border region of *aloka*, those lying within its intermediate region, all the substances taken together, the space-points lying in each one of these, and so on. The calculations are that the border regions of loka and aloka are respectively made of infinite substances and infinite-times infinite space-points, these being slightly more for *aloka* than for *loka*. The intermediate region of *loka* as well as *aloka* is made up of just one substance, whereas space-points are infinite for the *loka* and innumerable for *aloka*.

LOWER AND UPPER PARTS OF LOKA

The lower part which has the shape of a wine cup turned upside down, has seven hells in the following order: Ratnaprabha, Sarkaraprabha, Balukaprabha, Pankaprabha, Dhumaprabha, Tamahprabha and Mahatamahprabha. These have been called *bhumis* or regions. In between one region and another, there are spaces of unmeasured dimensions and a similar space-gap separates the Mahatamahprabha hell from *aloka*. Each region, again, is enveloped by hulls which, in succession, consist of viscous water (*ghano-dadhi*), viscous wind (*ghanovata*) and light wind (*tanu-vata*). Of the regions, the top-most entitled Ratnaprabha has three portions or *kandas* and a portion of this region falls in the central sphere. Here the line of demarcation becomes very thin.

According to the earlier view, the denigens of hells are human beings who undergo punishments in certain allotted places in the hells, in the infernal rivers and mountains. Later views, however, consider these denigens as a distinct species who are called *nerayias* or *narakiyas* who are dark and ghastly, sexless, emitting a smell of decay, and causing pain when being touched. They vary greatly in size, are in inconstant suffering from hunger and thirst, from heat and cold, and live in mutual suspicion and dread. In the uppermost hell a part of which falls in the central sphere, some species of gods reside called the *bhanavasis* and the *vanavyantaras*. The *vanavyantaras* provide a link with the central sphere.

The upper sphere comprising the various heavens has various layers, more in number than in the case of the lower sphere, which are arranged one above another, till one reaches the highest which is occupied by the liberated souls. The upper sphere begins at an altitude immeasurably high above the planetary bodies. There, separated from each other by intervening space, different portions of the upper sphere lie one above another. These interspaces are covered by hulls of viscous water and viscous wind. The lowest celestial regions called *kalpas* consist of Saudharma and Aisana which lie on the same level above the viscous water hull. Above them, and beyond the viscous wind hull lie Mahendra and Sanat-kumara, again in pair. According to Umasvati, however, there are no pairs, each heaven lying one above another, Aisana above Saudharma and so on. Above them lie singly, one above another, Brahmaloka, Lantaka, Mahasukra and Sahasrara. Then again, in pairs, the four uppermost heavens, Pranata paired with Anata, and Acyuta with Arana. The twelve *kalpas* end at this point. These are inhabited by the *kalpotpanna devas* (gods born in heavens), and each heaven has its Indra who is the leader and king of the gods. They visit the human part of the sphere, if and when necessary. Above the *kalpas* are located the lower, intermediate and upper *graiveyakas* (so called because their location looks like a neck). They are inhabited by superior gods each one of whom is an Indra (*ahamindra*). These never come out of their abodes. Above them, and just beneath the world of the liberated beings, there are the five *anuttara vimanas* (so called because there are no *vimanas* beyond them), all on one level.*

WORLD OF ANIMALS AND MEN

The world of animals and men is located in the central sphere because of which it should be the most important to us. It is the central sphere, again, which has dominated over all the conventional views on cosmology, western as well as eastern, till the time of the Copernican revolution. From the spiritual point of view, too, the central sphere should be significant, since located here is the land of spiritual action (*karmabhumi*) as distinguished from the land of experiences (*bhogabhumi*). In the latter, the outcome of *karma*, good as well as bad, is experienced, but it is not possible to take any step for redress, which is possible only in the land of action. The land of action is the necesssry base for going to the world of liberated souls. It is for this reason that this portion of the central sphere is even coveted of the gods.

The centre of interest in the central sphere is the Jambu-dvipa, so called because of the dominance of *jambu* (berry) trees all over the continent. Jambu-dvipa is surrounded on all sides by an enclosure which has numerous window-like openings, some small, but four of them in four directions which are big enough to be called gates. The rivers Sita and Sitoda fall into the eastern and the western gates, since they provide entrance to the Lavana *samudra* (Salt sea). Beyond the Lavana *samudra*, we have the isle called Dhatakikhanda which is encircled by Kalodadhi sea. The Kalodadhi sea, in turn, is encircled by the isle named Puskara. Through the Puskara island runs, bangle-like, the Manusottara mountain dividing the island into the inner and the outer halves. With Jambu-dvipa, Dhatakikhanda and inner half of Puskara, the world of men ends. At this point terminate all human ideas and standards including chronology and time-sense, because of which this region consisting of two and a half isles is alternately called *samaya-ksetra*. Even atmospheric

---

* For details, Walther Schubring, *The Doctrine of the Jainas,*

phenomenon like lightning, thunder, rainfall, cease at this point, and fire, minerals, darkness and even astronomical phenomena do not appear. Beyond this point, there is hardly anything of human interest, and if still a few more islands and seas are mentioned, it is just to complete the picture of the central sphere. These are Puskara sea encircling the Puskara isle, and itself encircled by Varunavara isle, which in turn is encircled by Varunavara sea, which in turn is encircled by Ksiravara isle, which in turn is encircled by Ghrtavara isle, which in turn is encircled by Ghrtoda sea, which in turn is encircled by Iksuvara isle, which in turn is surrounded by Iksuda sea, and then the Nandisvara isle and the Nandisvara sea, and so on, there being many isles and many seas, the last one being Svayambhuramana isle and Svayambhuramana sea. And there the central sphere ends. Therefore, it should appear that the world of animals and of men is only a fraction of the central sphere comprising of two seas and two and a half isles. The gods in the central sphere are the sun, the moon, the planets, the *naksatras* and the *prakirna* stars. Their movements are restricted to the *samayaksetra*, i.e., upto the Manusottara mountain, and beyond this, they have no movement. There are many suns and many moons in the region, Jambu-dvipa itself being served by two suns and two moons. The logic that is advanced is that in the course of 24 hours, the sun can complete not more than half its circle round Mount Meru which is the pivot. Now, when it is day in the northern sphere, there is also day in the southern sphere, and this is not possible unless there are two suns. And by the same logic, there are two moons over Jambu-dvipa.

GEOGRAPHY OF JAMBUDVIPA

Jambudvipa is located at the centre of the central sphere. Mount Meru stands at the centre of this isle. Jambudvipa is divided into seven zones, viz., Bharatavarsa, Haimavatavarsa, Harivarsa, Videhavarsa, Ramyakvarsa, Hairanyavatavarsa and Airavatavarsa, each separated from the other by a 'world' mountain running from the east to the west. These world mountains are called Himavan, Mahahimavan, Nisadha, Nila, Rukmi and Sikhari. Mount Meru is to the north of all the *varsas*, i.e., to the left-hand side if one is to face the sun.

Videhavarsa, Mahavideha or simply Videha is at the centre

of the seven *varsas*. It has two parts, Purva-Videha which is to the east of Mount Meru, and Avara-Videha which is to its west. Each part is divided into sixteen *vijayas*. To the south and to the north of Mount Meru, there are located Devakuru and Uttarakuru. The world mountains shelter at an altitude large lakes from which originate the river systems. From the lakes on the Himavan and the Sikhari, there flow three rivers each,—into Bharatavarsa flow the Ganga in the east and the Sindhu in the west, and northward, into Haimavatavarsa flows the Rohitasya; in the Airavatavarsa, the Rakta in the east, the Raktoda in the west, and northward into Hiranyavatavarsa flows the Suvarnakula. From the remaining lakes spring two rivers each to flow southward and northward. All these fall into the Lavana sea. Each of the two rivers in Bharatavarsa and two in Airavatavarsa has five tributaries. The tributaries of the Ganga are the Yamuna, the Sarayu, the Adi, the Kosi and the Mahi, and those of the Sindu are the Satadru, the Vitasta, the Vipasa, the Iravati and the Candrabhaga. On the slope of Mount Meru, we have four forests.

Jambudvipa has 7 *varsas*, Dhatakikhanda has 14 and so also Puskara has 14, a total of 35. Of these, only 15 are land of action where *tirthankaras* are born to propound *dharma*. Of these, five are in Bharatavarsa, five in Airavatavarsa and five in the Videhas.

Bharatavarsa is located in the southern part of Jambudvipa, and is called after King Bharata, son of the first *tirthankara* Adinatha Risabha. The country is like a crescent in shape, bounded in the north by the Himavan mountain, and on the other three sides by the Lavana sea. Its length north to south is 526 *yojanas* 6 *kalas*, and east to west 14,472 *yojanas* 6 *kalas* and area 53,80,681 *yojanas* 17 *kalas* 17 *vikalas*. The Vaitadhya mountain runs through the heart of Bharatavarsa dividing the country into two halves, north India and south India. The Ganga and the Sindhu pass through the Vaitadhya mountain, and fall into the sea, thus dividing the northern half of the country into three parts and also the southern half into three parts.

ATMOSPHERIC AND OTHER PHENOMENA

The *Bhagavati Sutra* has an exhaustive list of atmospheric phenomena in the words of Mahavira. The occasion was provided by discussion on the Lokapalas (who are the overlords of the directions) of Sakra, the Indra of the gods, their king, and the language is overwhelmingly mythological. But a careful reader may detect the various atmospheric phenomena refered to therein. The account given in Mahavira's words is as follows:

> *All the activities that take place to the south of Mount Meru in this Jambu-dvipa, such as graha-danda, grahamu-sala, graha-garjita, graha-yuddha, graha-sringataka, graha-pasavya, avra, avra-briksa, sandhya, gandharva-nagara, shower of meteors, burning of directions, uproar, lightning, shower of dust, yupa, yaksoddipta, dhumika, mahika, rajodghata, lunar eclipse, solar eclipse, candra parivesa, surya parivesa, prati-candra, prati-surya, rain-bow, udaka-matsya, kapihasita, amogha, wind from the eastern direction, wind from the westen direction, till samvartaka wind, burning of villages, till burning of sannivesa, destruction of life, destruction of people, destruction of wealth, destruction of race, till famine, sinful acts, and all acts of this nature are not unknown to Maharaja Soma, the Lokapala of Sakra; they are not unseen by him; they are not unheard of by him; they are not unremembered by him; they are not particularly unknown to him.*

The activities coming within the purview of Lokapala Yama have been stated to be as follows:

> obstructions, troubles created by the princes, quarrels, exchanges of words, hatred, great wars, great battles, hurling of great weapons, death of great personalities, bloodshed, existence of wicked people, diseases of *mandala*, urban diseases, eye-soar, ear-ache, ache in the nail, tooth-ache, *indra-graha, skanda-graha, kumara-graha, yaksa-graha,* fever on alternate days, fever at a gap of two days, four days, restlessness, cough, breathing trouble, debility fever, typhoid, sore on body-parts like arm-pit, indigestion, jaundice, piles, fistula, acute pain in the heart, in the brain, in the uteras, in the hips, in the arm-pits, village epidemic, town epidemic, till *sannivesa* epidemic, destruction of race, famines, sinful activities, etc., etc.

The activities coming within the purview of Lokapala Varuna have been stated to be as follows:

> heavy rain, mild rain, balanced rain, unbalanced rain, water-springs lakes, streams, rivers, flooding of villages, till of *sannivesa*, loss of life, etc., etc.

The activities coming within the purview of LokapalaV aisramana have been stated to be as follows:

> iron mines, zinc mines, copper mines, lead mines, silver mines, gold mines, diamond mines, *vajra-ratna* mines, drizzles of wealth, of silver, of gold, of gems, of thunder, of ornaments, of leaves, of flowers, of fruits, of seeds, of wreaths, of colours, of powders, of perfumes, of clothes, showers of silver, of gold, of gems, of *vajra-ratna*, of leaves, of flowers, of fruits, of seeds, of wreaths, of colours, of powders, of perfumes, of clothes, of vessels, of milk, good time, bad time, low price, high price, easy begging, difficult begging, purchase, sale and stock of *ghee*, jaggery, etc., stock of corn, of treasure, of wealth, treasure whose owners are dead, etc., etc., till treasure hidden in cremation ground, beneath city sewerage, on hills, in caves, in *santi-griha*, in a cavern curved out of a mountain, in assembly halls or in residential buildings.
>
> —*Bhagavati Sutra*, S. 3, U. 7

Some of these phenomena are man-made, but most others are made by natural agencies, and hence are beyond human power., This account as given by Mahavira is rich in terminology, and if suitably adopted, may enrich our own vocubulary.

IN CHAPTER 15, we had a discussion on *jiva* or the Jaina theory of
of the soul. The soul, however, makes its existence through a body
in which it is sheltered. The Jainas have identified 563 body-types
among 24 species of beings. Not many of these body-types
are known to modern biological sciences. The following discussion
will show that the Jaina contribution to biological sciences is not
only the earliest, but also most strikingly original.

GENERAL CONSIDERATIONS

All material things including the body of an organism are ultimately
produced by the combination of atoms. Two atoms form a compound when the one is viscous and the other dry, or both are of
different degrees of viscousness and dryness. Such compounds
combine with others, and are in the process of constant change and
transformation of qualities.

Bodies differ according as they have been acquired in one or
other existence, according as they have been created from an embryo,
egg or otherwise, according as they are with full attainments or
without full attainments, or according as they have one, two, three,
four or five sense organs. The Jaina notion about beings with only
one organ is peculiar to themselves, and they have seen life everywhere including earth, water, air, fire, etc. These may be called
elementary lives, but to call this an 'animistic idea' as Jacobi has done
is not correct. These elementary lives live and die and are born
again in a similar or some other elementary body. These elementary
lives may be gross or subtle; in the latter case, they are invisible.

These elementary lives do not occur in the same way everywhere
in the world, but we find them in all its three sections. They represent the palpable occurence of its elements, and to mention but
some of them, they appear in the form of earth, minerals and metals;
of water, cloud and snow; of flame, coal and lightning; of breath,
wind and storm. The animate elements of earth, water and wind
appear in a concrete shape, except in the central world, at all obvious
places also within the sphere of the subterranean and heavenly
dwellings and naturally, also, in the structure of the hulls enveloping

the lower world. In the watery hulls, there are also concrete vegetable bodies with souls. Fire is confined to the central world as far
as it is inhabited by men. Fire comes to glow only when joined by
the wind. The lower and the higher animals occur in the lower and
the central world.

The last class of one-organ lives, as stated above, are plants.
Some of these have only one soul, and some an aggregation of
souls. Examples of the latter are lichens, mosses, etc, without any
subdivision, but very rich in variety. The aggregation of embodied
souls have all functions of life, including respiration and nutrition,
in common. That plants have soul is an opinion shared by other
Indian philosophers; but the Jainas have developed this theory in a
remarkable way. Plants in which only one soul is embodied are
always gross; they exist in the habitable parts of the world only.
But those plants of which each is a colony of several souls may also
be subtle, and, in consequence, invisible, and these are distributed
all over. These subtle plants are called *nigoda;* they are composed
of an infinite number of souls forming a very small cluster, and they
experience the most exquisite pains. Innumerable *nigodas* form a
globule, and with them the whole space of the world is closely
packed., like a box filled with powder. The *nigodas* furnish the
supply of souls in place of those who have been liberated. A single
nigoda has almost an infinite capacity to fill the world with life,
and, with the *nigoda* as the source of supply of souls, the world
will never be empty of living beings.

The more highly developed individual plants are placed into
12 types, such as, trees, bushes, shrubs, creepers, grasses, etc. Trees
are divided into two groups as mono-kernels and multi-kernels.
With its quality to have more than one soul, the latter stands in the
world of living beings. The seats of these souls are the roots, the
bulb, the stem, the bark, the branches, the twigs, the leaves, the
blossoms, the fruits and the seeds. The intake of matter and its
absorption starts with the souls of the roots which are near to the
souls of the earth from where they take whatever sustenance they
need. From the roots, they are taken to the bulbs and elsewhere.
The rainy season is the most congenial for the growth of plant life.

A being comes into existence physically in either of the three
ways, by manifestation, by coagulation or by generation. Manifestation means creation brought about with lightning-like suddenness

12

without any material basis. The infernal and the celestial beings
are born thus. Coagulation takes place spontaneously out of existing matter; it pertains to all beings with one to four sense organs.
All higher animals and human beings come into existence partly
in the same way and partly by generation.

EMBRYOLOGY

In giving reply to various questions raised by Indrabhuti Gautama,
Mahavira gave out many things on embryo life. Nearly always,
these are concerned with human life. Quoted below are Mahavira's
own statements as they occur in the *Bhagavati Sutra* (S. 1., U. 7):

> *To some extent, the embryo is with organs of senses and
> to some extent it is without organs of senses. As for objec-
> tive organs, it is without organs of senses; as for subjective,
> it is with organs of senses.*
>
> *From the standpoint of gross, fluid and assimilative body,
> it is without a body; but from the standpoint of caloric
> and karman body, it is with a body.*
>
> *Its first intake is the mother's blood and the father's semen—
> kalusa and kilvisa,—which are the first intake on entering
> the mother's womb ... Along with ·the mother's blood,
> the embryo takes a part of the substances from the mother's
> multifarious intakes.*
>
> *The intake and its transformation that the soul has after
> being lodged in the womb go in straight to form its organ
> of touch, bones, marrows, hairs, beard, pore-hairs, and
> nails. Hence the embryo has no stool, urine, phlegm, nose
> dirt, vomitting and bile.*

Throwing further light on intake. Mahavira said,

> *The soul lodged in the womb has intake by its whole frame,
> transforms it by its whole frame, inhales by its whole frame,
> exhales by its whole frame, has intake very often, trans-
> formation very often, etc. ... And then there is a tissue
> sprouting from the mother which derives the elixir from the
> mother, and supplies it to the child, and this is linked with
> the mother's vital organ, and this also touches the child. With
> this tissue, the child derives intake and transforms it. There*

is another tissue which issues forth from the child's vital organ and touches the mother. This helps the child in the absorption and assimilation of the intake.

Regarding the elements acquired by the embryo from his parents, he said,

> *The contributions of the mother's limbs have been stated to be three, viz., flesh, blood and brain. The contributions of the father's limbs have been stated to be three, viz., bones and marrows, hairs including beard and porehairs, and nails. These acquired from the parents stick to the soul as long as its earthly body exists. And then as the earthly body becomes lean in course of time due to the impact of age, and ultimately ends, the elements acquired from the parents' bodies also end.*

On life in the mother's womb, Mahavira has something important to say, which is as follows:

> *A being lodged in the womb lies on the back, on his sides; he lies with a curve like a mango; he lies in his normal shape, . . . sleeps when the mother sleeps, and wakes when the mother wakes . . . is sad when the mother is sad. If he comes out by the head or by the legs, that's the right posture. If he comes out by the side, he dies. If his karma is affixed in an inauspicious manner, . . . then such one is born with bad shape, bad hue, etc. But if his karma is not affixed in an inauspicious manner, then, all the aforesaid items are reversed.*

ANATOMY OF HUMAN BODY

Complete anatomy of human body has been given, and so the structure of the body, its shape, its size, bodily functions like breathing, speech, etc. Life has ten stages or *dasas*. The second of the sequence indicates a decline of the senses, loquacity, bending of the body, expectation of death and then death itself. The appointment of these ten stages goes back to the theory of assuming a maximum age of 100 years. Half of this time is spent in sleeping, and another 20 years for childhood and old age, so that the effective part of life is no more than 30 years, or it may even be less depending on the expectation of life.

The margin of fertility is 55 years with a woman and 75 with man, and the embryo remains in the womb for 277½ days in normal cases. Its stages are listed as *kalala, aubbuya, pesi* and *ghana.* Its weight amounts to 3 *karisa* which is equal to 3/4 *pala* in the first month, in the second it gets solid, in the third it rouses lusts within the mother, in the fourth it makes the mother's limbs swell, in the fifth its extremities and head take shape, in the sixth its gall and its blood, in the seventh its veins, muscles, vessels, nerves, pores, hairs and nails, and in the eighth month the child is complete. The sex depends on the preponderance of either sperm or blood; in the case neither prevails, the child is impotent or sexless. A sexless fruit lies in the centre of the mother, a male on the right side and a female on the left. Are not these informations very modern?

Physical death is scarcely referred to, since there is no such thing as death in the Jaina view. We are merely told that the soul leaves the body simultaneously by its feet, its thighs, its chest, its head, and all its limbs. Thereafter it will remain either in hell, among animals, among men of gods, or it will enter into the realm of the perfected souls.

In the Light of the Prajnapana Sutra

The *Bhagavati* has made many references to the biological stand of the Jainas. Not only does it evince a keen awareness of the peculiarity of the Jaina stand, but frequently seeks to reassure the reader that the position is nevertheless valid. A more detailed and developed consideration exists in the *Prajnapana Sutra* in which, leaving aside portions of some chapters dealing with *loka-aloka,* etc., and about six chapters discussing the *karma* theory, the rest of it is devoted to presenting the Jaina view of organism. The items discussed are catalogued in a chapterwise sequence without, however, providing the details for want of space.

Chapter one entitled *Prajnapanapada* gives necessary information about organism. It presents an elaborate classification of the animate world including the five species of one organ beings. Chapter two entitled *Sthanapada* gives information about the geographical distribution of living beings. Chapter three entitled *Alpa-vahutva-pada* considers the numerical strength of different species of beings.

Chapter four entitled *Sthitipada* deals with the spans of life for different classes of beings. Though some of the accounts have high mythological undertones, they are undoubtedly very methodical. Chapter three has, in addition, a novel scheme of classification of living beings on the basis of 20 items which the Svetamvaras have called *marganasthanas*. Chapter five entitled *Visesapada* discusses the comparability of two souls at a point of time and has introduced eight items on which comparison is feasible. Chapter thirteen entitled *Parinamapada* contains an enumeration of the basic properties of the soul which are stated to be ten, viz., class, sense organs, passions, tinges, activities, cognition, knowledge, vision, conduct, experience. With these the general considerations about a living being end.

The rest of the *Sutra* discusses the various activities of a living being. Although the details of these activities are not relevant for our purpose here, broadly, it may be stated, these fall under five heads, viz., physical, cognitive, emotive, conative and affective. With so much detail, hardly any aspect of the life of an organism will be missing. With a spiritual purpose, the Jainas, in fact, enumerated biological sciences and attained a level which is high for all times. The following comparative study will substantiate the point.

WESTERN BIOLOGICAL SCIENCES: A COMPARISON

The earliest discussion on organism appears in Aristotle who was junior to Mahavira. His consideration falls under three heads:

1. on psyche or what he calls *de anima*;
2. on its history (*historia annimalium*); and
3. on the origin of psyche (*de partibus animalium*).

The earliest meaning of the word 'psyche' is the sense of respiration or breathing which distinguishes the living from the non-living. Living beings have been classified by Aristotle into three types as vegetable souls, animal souls and rational (human) souls. Of these, vegetable souls have been considered to be the lowest. They have two traits, viz., growth and capacity to reproduce. In contrast, animal souls have three, power of movement added, and rational souls have four, including power of judgement which guides all their activities and movements. To Aristotle, man stands

out as the highest soul. Aristotle said nothing about the infernal
and celestial beings about which Mahavira has said at great length.
Regarding the relation of psyche with the living body, Aristotle
has written,

> They are right who hold the soul as not independent of
> the body and yet as not in itself anything of the nature
> of the body. It is not body but something belonging to
> body. It, therefore, resides in body, and moreover a par-
> ticular soul to a particular body. They were wrong who
> sought to fit the soul into the body without regard to the
> nature and qualities of that body. For the *entelechy*
> comes naturally to be developed in the potentiality of
> each thing and it is manifest that soul is a certain *entelechy*
> and notional form of that which has the capacity to be
> endowed with soul.

In other words, according to Aristotle, any soul cannot live in
any body; it lives in a particular body. This is not dissimilar from
the Jaina view in which the quality of the body a soul takes depends
upon its *karma*; it cannot make a blind selection of the body. A soul
which is fit to acquire a human body does not live in the body of
a bug or a flora. This is the implication of the word *entelechy* for
which the nearest English synonym would be 'in-dwelling purposi-
veness'. Had Aristotle stopped at this point, there would not have
been much difficulty for the Jaina philosophers to lend their support
to him. But he says something more which is not acceptable to the
Jainas.

Aristotle has, in the beginning, distinguished the rational soul
from the animal and the vegetable, but later he says that the distinction is not absolute. If the animal soul develops rationality, the
difference may be wiped out. Read, for instance,

> Nature proceeds little by little, from things lifeless to
> animal life in such a way that it is impossible to determine
> the exact line of demarcation, nor on which side thereof
> an intermediate form should lie. Thus next after lifeless
> things in the upward scale comes the plant . . . There is in
> plants a continuous scale of ascent towards the animal
> . . . Thus nature passes from lifeless objects to animals

in unbroken sequence so that scarcely any difference seems to exist between two neighbouring groups by reason of their close similarity.

Here the phrase 'a continuous state of ascent' is important. For, later biologists have interpreted it in terms of the evolution of species, on which the mature product is Charles Darwin's *Origin of Species* published in 1859. The Jainas, too, believe in evolution, but an ape kept under observation for a thousand years will not turn into a man. The Jainas have envisaged 84 *lakh* body-types, and the soul acquires one or the other depending on its *karma*. If the soul improves its status, there is nothing to prevent it to acquire the most developed body type; if, on the other hand, it is bogged in demerit, nothing can prevent its going to the *nadir* of perdition. The Jainas thus do not believe in the steady ascent upward, but pin their faith in the agency of *karma*, which determines where the soul is to be lodged.

There is another important point of difference between the Jainas and the western biological sciences, For, whereas the Jainas believe that both soul and matter are eternal, according to the western scientists, the soul is not eternal, it appears at a certain point in time when atmospheric conditions make the existence of life possible, and it is possible, therefore, to produce life in a lab. With these suppositions, the western scientists hold that matter which alone is eternal is in the continuous process of transformation, and that at a certain stage in this transformation, organism makes its appearance. Efforts are, therefore, afoot to prove that life can be created in a lab. If some day science succeeds, it may be necessary to take a fresh look at the Jaina view; but till then there is no reason to believe that the Jaina view stands exploded in any way.

GENERAL CONSIDERATIONS

ALL THE *astikayas* named by the Jainas except the *jiva* are inanimate, and with the single exception of matter, all the latter are immaterial. Materiality is defined by the Jainas by saying that among all inanimate fundamental facts, matter alone is palpable, whereas this does not apply to motion, rest or space, even though they fill the world completely. Betwen soul and matter, both are substances and both are plural rather than singular, being infinite in number and variety, and both are active in themselves. For, the nature of the soul rests in its intellecual function which, by means of will and skill, is put to use in all possibilities of intellectual cognition. Matter causes the soul to take possession of bodies and to perform bodily functions.

Logically, the masses are preceded by their parts and these have been called *desas* and *pradesas*. But while *pradesas* are essential for the structure of the world, the *desas* represent but calculable quantities. To illustrate, motion, rest and sky do not exist in their totality in the lower and upper and higher regions, but only in parts or *desas*, in the total universe, they do not exist in parts but in their whole, excepting, of course, the *akasa* (sky) which exists in the world as well as non-world. It is the *pradesas* or the space-points which in their totality constitute the masses.

Coming to matter, the Jainas have used the word *pudgala* to signify matter. As already said, matter is eternal and the only one among the substances that has a physical character. Owing to fineness, it eludes observation, but it possesses the qualities of colour, smell and taste. Matter exists in two forms, viz., atoms (*anu*) and aggregates (*skandha*). The Jainas begin with an absolutely homogeneous mass of *pudgalas*, which, by differentiation (*bheda*) break up into several kinds of atoms qualitatively determined, and integration by differentiation, integration and differentiation in the integrated form aggregates or *skandhas*. An *anu* has no parts, no beginning, middle or end. An *anu* is not only infinitesimal but also eternal and ultimate. A *skandha* may vary from being an aggregate of two's, three's and so on *ad infinitum*. The ascending grades are: (*i*) those which can be numbered called *samkheya*, (*ii*) those which are infinitely large and so cannot easily be numbered called *asamkheya*, (*iii*) infinity of the first order called *ananta*, (*iv*) infinity of the second order called *anantananta*, and so on.

The specific character of the *pudgalas* are of two kinds, viz., those which are found in atoms as well as in aggregates, and those which are found only in aggregates. Qualities of touch, taste, smell and colour come under the first head. The original *pudgalas* being homogeneous and indeterminate, all sensible qualities are the result of evolution (*parinama*). According to this theory, therefore, earth atoms, water atoms, etc., are but differentiations of originally homogeneous matter. An aggregate of two's, three's or of higher order possess, in addition to touch, taste, etc., the following physical characters, viz., sound, atomic linking or mutual attraction and repulsion of atoms, dimension, figure, divisiblility, opacity and casting of shadows, and radiant heat and light.

The most remarkable contribution of the Jainas to the atomic theory relates to their analysis of atomic linking or repulsion of atoms in the formation of molecules. On this part of the Jaina theory, Sir P. C. Ray writes:

> The Jainas hold that the different classes of elementary substances (*bhutas*) are all evolved from the same primordial atoms. . . . The linking takes place under different conditions. Ordinarily speaking, one particle of matter (*pudgala*) must be negative, and the other positive (*visama-guna-yukta*): the two particles must have two peculiar opposite qualities, . . . to make the linking possible. But the linking takes place where the qualities, though opposed, are very feeble (*jaghanya*). Ordinarily speaking, two homogeneous particles, i.e., both positive or both negative do not unite. This is the case where the opposite qualities are equal in intensity. But if the strength or intensity of one is twice as great as that of the other, or exceeds that portion, then even similar particles may be attracted towards each other. In every case, a change of state in both the particles is supposed to be the result of this linking, and the physical characters of this aggregate depend on the nature of this linking. When particles of equal intensity (negative and positive) modify each

other, there is mutual action; in case of unequal intensity, the higher intensity transforms the lower ... All changes in the qualities of atoms depend on this linking. The *Tattvarthadhigama* of Umasvati which expounds this theory most probably dates back to the first half of the first century A.D.

—P. C. Ray, *History of Hindu Chemistry,*

Vol. II, p. 178-83

IN THE LIGHT OF THE BHAGAVATI SUTRA

In giving reply to a question by Indrabhuti Gautama, Mahavira said,

> Matter existed in the past from an endless, eternal time; matter exists in the present from an endless, eternal time; matter will continue to exist in the future for an endless, eternal time. And all the three, i.e., past, present and future are relevant of the cluster of matter-atoms, as all the three are relevant of the souls.   (S. 1., U. 4)

On the relation between soul and matter, Mahavira said,

> Soul and matter are tied to one another, touched by one another, in deep tie with one another, affixed to one another as if by glue, are compounded with one another. (S. 1, U. 6)

In giving reply to a question whether matter is heavy, light, or otherwise, Mahavira said,

> Matter is not heavy, nor light, but heavy-light, also non-heavy non-light. Relative to heavy-light objects, matter is neither heavy nor light, nor non-heavy non-light, but heavy-light; relative to non-heavy non-light objects, matter is neither heavy, nor light, nor heavy-light, but non-heavy non-light.   (S. 1, U. 9)

In refuting the views of the heretics regarding the formation of aggregates, Mahavira said,

> Two matter atoms stick to each other ... because there are minute water-bodies between the two; if divided they

*make two ... Three matter atoms stick to one another ...
If divided, there may be two divisions, and also three divisions. With two divisions, there is one matter atom in one
part, and a bunch of two making a skandha in the other.
... That five matter atoms stick to one another; and by
sticking to one another, they make a skandha; and that
skandha is transcient, and it waxes and wanes.* (S. 1, U. 10)

Sataka 5 *Uddesaka* 7 of the *Bhagavati* have many things to
say on matter atoms. Both as units and as aggregates, they throb
sometimes, and sometimes they do not. The matter atoms cannot
be divided. Even the sharpest weapon has no effect on them. But
skandhas with infinite *pradesas* can be pierced and divided when
they are of coarse variety. They cannot be divided when they are
fine. Atoms are the smallest part of matter which can neither be
divided, nor crushed or powdered.

When *skandhas* have an even number of *pradesas*, say, two,
four, six, etc., they are said to be *sardha* and *amadhya*. When they
have an odd number of *pradesas*, they are said to be *samadhya*
and *anardha*. *Skandhas* with limited, unlimited and infinite *pradesas*
may have either an odd number or an even number of *pradesas*.

When matter exists in the form of a *skandha* with, say, two
pradesas, it is matter as substance. When it exists on one or more
pradesas of space, it is matter as place. When it exists in some shape
or form, it is matter as shape or form. In other words, life-span as
substance (*dravya-sthanayu*), life-span as place (*ksetra-sthanayu*),
life-span as shape (*avagahana-sthanayu*) and life-span as phenomena
(*bhava-sthanayu*) characterise individual atom as well as aggregate.

There are many such passages in the *Bhagavati* showing the
deep interest taken by Mahavira and his disciples in the atomic
theory of matter, and the penetrating analysis given by them. Till
perhaps the 1st century A.D., the Jainas sought to develop the
atomic theory of which atomic linking was a mature outcome, and
thereafter they did not pursue it further.

IN THE LIGHT OF THE PRAJNAPANA SUTRA*

Chapter one of the *Prajnapana* lays down the following qualities
of matter: 5 colours, 5 tastes, 2 smells, 8 touches and 5 shapes.

Based on K. K. Dixit, *Ontology*, Ahmedabad, 1971, pp. 43-50.

Chapter 13 adds the following to the aforesaid list: speech (*sabda*), binding (*bandha*), motion (*gati*), splitting (*bheda*) and non-heavy non-lightness (*aguru-laghutva*). That speech is made of atoms is an old Jaina position. One whole chapter (Chap. 11) is devoted to speech. 'Binding' describes the process of atomic linking. 'Motion' is classified into long and short, and touch-producing and non-touch-producing. Under the heading 'splitting' are described the five ways in which a physical body might disintegrate. 'Non-heavy non-lightness' characterise certain types of physical substance.

Chapter 5 enumerates the counts on which two physical bodies might be compared with each other, and a list of 5 items has been drawn as follows:

(*i*)   being a substance;

(*ii*)   possessing *pradesas;*

(*iii*)   possessing a size (in terms of *akasa pradesas*);

(*iv*)   possessing a duration (in terms of *addha-samaya*); and

(*v*)   possessing a property or mode (in terms of *bhava*).

Two physical bodies are equivalent as substance, but they may differ in respect of possessing constituent atoms, size, duration and degree of property. Accordingly, the following six positions have been reached:

(*i*)   y may be more or less than x by an amount equivalent to x/*samkhyata.*

(*ii*)   y may be more or less than x by an amount equivalent to x/*asankhyata.*

(*iii*)   y may be more or less than x by an amount equivalent to x/*ananta.*

(*iv*)   y may be equivalent to x/*samkhyata* or x-times *samkhyata.*

(*v*)   y may be equivalent to x/*asamkhyata* or x-times *asamkhyata.*

(*vi*)   y may be equivalent to x/*ananta* or x-times *ananta.*

Chapter 3 entitled *Alpa-vahutvapada* gives the relative weight of physical bodies lying in the three worlds, and also in the ten directions. The same question has been raised of physical bodies made up of this or that number of constituent atoms, those occupying this or that number of space-points, those occupying this or that number of time-units, and those possessing this or that mode or property.

Chapter 10 entitled *Caramapada* discusses a technical question as to how the features *carama*, *acarama* and *avaktavya* are exhibited by physical bodies in their capacity as atomic aggregates. *Carama* atom is an atom lying in the border region, *acarama* atom lies in the intermediate region and *avaktavya* atom is indescribable either way. These features may appear singly, in two's or all together; and each one of these may appear in one part of the concerned body or in more than one part of it. Thus conceived, these features can appear singly in six ways, in two's in twelve ways and all the three together in eight ways, as follows:

APPEARING SINGLY	MINIMUM NUMBER OF ATOMS
1. one *carama*	2
2. one *acarama*	
3. one *avaktavya*	1
4. many *caramas*	
5. many *acaramas*	
6. many *avaktavyas*	

APPEARING IN TWO'S

1. one *carama* one *acarama*	5
2. one *carama*, many *acaramas*	6
3. many *caramas*, one *acarama*	3
4. many *caramas*, many *acaramas*	4
5. one *carama*, one *avaktavya*	3
6. one *carama*, many *avaktavyas*	4
7. many *caramas*, one *avaktavya*	5
8. many *caramas*, many *avaktavyas*	6
9. one *acarama*, one *avaktavya*	
10. one *acarama*, many *avaktavyas*	
11. many *acaramas*, one *avaktavya*	
12. many *acaramas*, many *avaktavyas*	

APPEARING IN THREE'S

1. one *carama*, one *acarama*, one *avaktavya*	6
2. one *carama*, one *acarama*, many *avaktavyas*	7

3. one *carama*, many *acaramas*, one *avaktavya*   7
4. one *carama*, many *acaramas*, many *avaktavya*   8
5. many *caramas*, one *acarama*, one *avaktavya*   4
6. many *caramas*, one *acarama*, many *avaktavyas*   5
7. many *caramas*, many *acaramas*, one *avaktavya*   5
8. many *caramas*, many *acaramas*, many *avaktavyas*   6

MATTER IN WESTERN PHILOSOPHY

For a comparative study, we may have a look at matter in Western philosophy. The earliest to discuss it were the Greek philosophers who were called the 'physicists'. They discarded the mythological views of their generation, and substituted instead views which they themselves arrived at by reflection upon physical environment. They were of opinion that there was some sort of ultimate stuff of which different objects in the physical environment are composed, and by reference to which events and changes in this environment could be accounted for. But they differed widely as to what this stuff was. Two significant points emerged from the early Greek thought which were that matter was really a group of elements, and that these elements were to be described in quantitative rather than qualitative terms. These views were further developed by Plato and Aristotle. According to Plato, various objects in physical environment were copies of general types or forms. The general type which the particular object copied was called 'idea', and the special characteristics of a given object arose from the material out of which the object was made. This material is called 'matter'. Thus 'precious stone' is the type or idea of which 'diamond' is a particular copy. But Plato could throw no further light on what matter was. Aristotle sought to explain matter in terms of the change noticeable in an object which was determined by something inherent within it as a sort of potentiality or capacity. In other words, in Aristotle's view, matter became synonymous with a capacity or potentiality to change. This view was later to influence European thinking on matter in a profound way.

After a gap of about two thousand years, matter was taken up for discussion by the European philosophers in the 15th and 16th centuries. Thus Descartes identified an important characteristic in matter which is extension. To Locke, matter was no more than a quality which was manifest in an object. This explanation was questioned by Berkeley who strongly denied that matter was something mysterious and unknown lying behind qualities, and asserted with a certain amount of force that matter was a name we gave to the totality of objects in physical environment. But these objects are nothing but a collection of various qualities. So matter came to stand for the qualities of objects. Leibnitz was very much influenced by the Greek thinkers and was, therefore, unwilling to admit that matter elements had any spatial characteristics. His logic was that these elements to be ultimates must have no extension. To him, therefore, matter became a non-extended centre of force or energy, which he called 'monad'. Since there are many objects in physical environment, there must be many monads. Thus for Leibnitz, matter became an indefinite number of centres of activity (monad) organised in such manifold ways as to constitute those various groups of qualities which we experience as physical objects.

In modern times, the atomic theory of matter suggested that matter is reducible to certain elements called atoms. John Dalton was one of the first among the scientists to make fairly definite suggestions concerning the atomic theory, and the measurable weights of some of the atoms. But the early assumption that each atom is simple in structure and impenetrable by further analysis is now rejected. Recent investigations, particularly in physics have led to the inference that each atom is within itself a complex universe of electrical energy. It is now said to be composed of positive electricity called 'nucleus' and one or more negative electricity called 'electrons' revolving about the nucleus at a very rapid rate of motion. Differences among atoms bear a definite and measurable ratio to differences in number and configurations of electrons composing them. Atoms are composite in structure and active in behaviour. It is a compound of rapidly revolving electrons whose numbers varied from atom to atom. It is electrical energy. It will thus be seen that the views of Mahavira on matter were very much advanced for his age and have not waned in significance in modern modern times. More research is, however, necessary in traditional physics.

To CONTINUE the thread of the previous chapter, in modern physics, matter has in the end been reduced to electricity. This obliterates the distinction between matter and energy. This does not seem to be very correct. Matter may be the home of energy, as it is the home of so many other things like taste, smell, touch, etc., but to call matter energy wipes out the very existence of matter as such. The Jainas, however, did not allow themselves to fall victim to a scientific trap, but steered clear of it. They have used the two words *dharma* and *adharma* to signify the media of motion and rest, and distinguished them from pure matter which they have called *pudgala*. Regarding *dharma* and *adharma*, we have the following line in the *Uttaradhyayana Sutra* (28.9);

> *gai-lakkhanou dhammo ahammo thana-lakkhano*

(The visible sign of *dharma* is motion, that of *adharma* rest.)   We have a more complete description of these in the *Bhagavati Sutra* (S. 2, U. 10) in part, as follows:

> *In dharmastikaya, there is no colour, no smell, no taste, no touch, no shape. It is non-living, eternal ever existent object in the sphere. In brief, dharmastikaya has been stated from five angles, viz., as substance, as place, as time, as phenomena, and as trait. As substance, dharmastikaya is one. As place, it is as extensive as the sphere. As time, it never was that it did not exist, it never is that it does not exist, nor will it ever be that it will not exist. It existed, it exists, it will exist ... till it is ever-existent object in the sphere. As phenomena, it has no colour, no taste, no touch. As trait, it is motion. Likewise, adharmastikaya, except that as trait, it is rest.*
>
> *Dharmastikaya is as big as the sphere, a replica of the sphere, with a similar expanse as the sphere, is touched by the sphere, and itself touches the sphere.   And like this adharmastikaya.*

On a further question by Indrabhuti Gautama, Mahavira made it clear without leaving any doubt that not one *pradesa* of *dharmasti-kaya*, nor many, constituted the whole of *dharmastikaya*, but all *pradesas* taken together constituted *dharmastikaya*. The dialogue is worth quoting:

> *Bhante ! Can it be said that one pradesa of dharmastikaya is the whole of dharmastikaya?*
> *Goyma ! This is not correct. Not even two, three, four, five, six, seven,eight, nine, ten pradesas are the whole of dharmastikaya.*

When Gautama asked why it was so, Mahavira, in his characteristic manner, said,

> *Goyama ! Is a part of a wheel the whole wheel?*
> *No, bhante ! It is not the whole wheel.*
> *The same with an umbrella, a cushion, a stick, cloth, a weapon and a sweet. Hence so. For this reason, it is said that a pradesa of dharmstikaya is not dharmastikaya, . . . till less than a pradesa of dharmastikaya is not dharma-stikaya.*

Mahavira concluded,

> *Dharmastikaya has innumerable pradesas: all of them, entire aggregate, leaving none out, the whole in one expres-sion,—such is dharmastikaya, and like this, too, adhar-mastikaya . . .*

Matter or *pudgala*, in the Jaina view, is something different. It is not only real, but also dynamic. We have the following in the *Naya-cakra-sara* by Devacandra,

> *purana-galana-svabhavah pudgalastikayah*

The term *pud* refers to the process of combination and *gala* stands for dissociation. Matter is said to be that which undergoes modifica-tions by combinations and dissociations. *Dharma*, in contrast, is the medium of motion, and pervades the whole universe. It must, however, be understood that the medium is not motion itself, but it helps those to move who have capacity to move. The medium of motion is an immaterial substance possessing no consciousness. Motion has none of the five sense qualities possessed by matter.

13

Existence is its nature, and hence it is not considered to be a product. From empirical standpoint, it is stated to possess an infinite number of space-points. Likewise *adharma*, except that it is the medium of rest and also pervades the whole universe. It is because of this that bodies in motion are enabled to enjoy a state of rest. It does not actively interfere with the moving object. In this respect, it is like the earth which provides the condition for rest for the living beings living on its surface. Like *dharma*, *adharma*, too, is considered to be devoid of sense qualities.

The idea of motion and rest, in clear distinction with that of matter, is an original contribution by the Jainas. Some have compared these with *rajah* and *tamah* in the Sankhya view, but the comparison is wrong and does not stand. The Jainas have considered *dharma* and *adharma* to be responsible for the systematic character of the universe. Without these two, there would be only chaos in the cosmos. If there is only motion and no rest, then, soul and matter would be moving all the while, and will never come to rest. If, on the contrary, there's only rest, soul and matter would remain static in space. In either case, the universe will not be a moving reality, and the word *jagat* (from the root *gam*) would lose its implication.

In European philosophy, the earliest to discover motion and rest were the physicists who were responsible for developing the atomic theory. It received further development in the hands of Descartes (born 1596). But the dichotomy did not resolve the basic problem which was one of 'continuity' when a thing was at rest, but started moving again. What was it that provided this continuity. This was Leibnitz's problem.

Leibnitz studied the presuppositions of the new science and found them inadequate. Even the facts of physics, he felt, could not be satisfactorily explained by the hypothesis of merely extended bodies and motion. Descartes had taught that the quantity of motion was constant, but bodies came to rest, and bodies began to move again. Thus there was a break. Motion was lost and gained afresh. This would vitiate the 'principle of continuity', the principle which means that Nature makes no leaps. There must be something that persists when motion ceases, the 'ground of motion'. This is Force or the Conatus, or the tendency of the body to move or to continue its motion. This is the most essential attribute of the body. Hence, the Law of Conservation of Motion was replaced by Leibnitz by the Law of Conservation of Force or Energy. Force to him was the fountain of the mechanical world. In the words of Leibnitz, "Extension presupposes in the body a property, attribute or nature that extends itself, spreads itself and continues itself." It is Force in the body that precedes all extension. It is owing to the Force in the body that it appears as matter. Every unit of Force is an indivisible union of soul and matter, activity and passivity; it is an organising, self-determining, purposive force that also limits itself and has the power of resistance.

According to Leibnitz, body is a plurality of simple Forces, which are 'metaphysical points', formal atoms, essential forms, substantial forms, what are called 'monads'. These points are true and real. Without them, nothing would be real. They are also eternal. They can neither be created nor destroyed. They are everywhere. The same principle that expresses itself in the mind of man is active in inanimate matter, in plant, in animal. There is Force everywhere. Each part of matter is like a garden full of plants. All matter is animate, alive, even to its minutest part. Needless to add, without attaining it, Leibnitz almost unknowingly came very near the Jaina stand.

Explaining his conception of 'monad', Leibnitz says that it is a universe in miniature, a microcosm, a 'living mirror of the universe'. But each monad represents the universe in its own way, from its unique point of view, with its characteristic degree of clearness. The higher the monad, the more clearly and distinctly it perceives, expresses or represents the world. From this it follows that

> everybody feels everything that occurs in the entire universe, so that anyone who sees all could read in each particular thing that which happens everywhere else, and, besides, all that has happened, and will happen, perceiving in the present that which is remote in time and space.
>
> —Leibnitz, *Monadology*, Sec. 61

Without beating about the bush so much, Mahavira comes straight to the point at issue and laid down that energy, activity and substance are at the root of the motion of the soul. Speaking of the conscious substance or the soul of the omniscient which, in the words of Leibnitz, is the highest of the monads, Mahavira laid it down very succinctly,

> *this soul is endowed with energy and activity because of which the limbs move. Now, the pradesas of the space which are occupied by the movement of hands and other limbs at the present time are not the same as the pradesas of the space that may be occupied in future by the movement of hands and other limbs because of which it is stated that the pradesas of the sky which are occupied at the present time by the movement of hands and other limbs are not the same as the pradesas of the sky that may be occupied in future by the movement of hands and other limbs.*
>
> —*Bhagavati Sutra*, S. 5, U. 4

In the above statement, there is an expression *viriyasayoga-saddavvyayae* which needs explanation. On the exhaustion of *karma* obstructing energy, this energy of the omniscient becomes unlimited so that mind and other organs of the body are full of energy; but till this is harnessed to some active use, there is no visible motion. Hence the word *sayoga*. Diverse interpretations have been given to *sat* in *saddavvyayae*. According to one, *sat* is *sattah* or existent; according to another, the substance called soul becomes *sat* with the removal of *karma* obstruction.

IN CHAPTER 24, we saw that in the western view, matter is identified
with energy so that it loses its separate identity. In Leibnitz, the
idea of matter is replaced by the idea of innumerable monads which
have different degrees of capacity. We have shown that without
falling into this sort of confusion, Mahavira could retain the separate
identity of matter, and yet could establish a consistent and convincing relation with the idea of motion and rest.

With the development of the idea of relativity in the west, matter
is now identified, not with energy, but with 'event', so that matter
is event. This is a new assault on the independent identity of matter
which, it is suggested, has been unavoidable because there is nothing
absolute in real life, and because everything is relative. But still
the most undeniable fact is that matter as such is one of the greatest
realities in the universe, the other one being souls. To merge it
either with energy or with events is simply atrocious. The Jainas
do not deny events, they do not deny energy, but they do not deny
matter as a separate identity either. In a dexterously produced
texture, Mahavira has clearly woven all the three, I mean, matter,
energy and event.

We start with a statement of western relativity which is fundamental. According to this, particular objects in our physical environment bear a spatial relation among themselves. Some may be
above, some below, some inside some outside, and so on. Such
relations are spatial. Spatial relation may, therefore, be defined
as apparent relation of position, size and shape among physical
objects.

Now, space may be of two types, viz., space of our perception
and space of our conception. Perceptual space is concerned with
distances between objects, their relative size, shape, location, etc.
Conceptual space is, in contrast, concerned with general concepts
of points, lines, surfaces, solids, etc., as we read in geometry or in
physics.

Like space, time is also perceptual and conceptual. Perceptual
time means those changes which we experience directly within
ourselves and around ourselves in the world of objects. Conceptual

time refers to a series of succession, one event following another, and successions are conceived as independent of events.

Now, both space and time may be singular as well as plural. Perceptual types are usually plural whereas conceptual types are singulars. The Jainas too have similar distinctions. Thus the word *kala* referring to eternal time is singular, while *samaya* which is perceptual time is invariably plural. Likewise, space in its entirety is singular in Jaina conceptiton, but *pradesas* or space-points are perceptual, and hence plural.

While space has three dimentions, length, breadth and depth, time has only one, viz., succession. Past, present and future are only three stages in a single, continuous flow of succession which runs in one direction only.

Space and time are characterised by three features. First, both are infinite meaning thereby that they have no conceivable end. In the Jaina view, space is finite in certain senses, and infinite in others. Second, both space and time are objective. But the Jaina refinement is that while space is an extended substance (*astikaya*), time is not. Third, which is a recent addition by mathematics and physics, both space and time are characterised by relativity. The Jaina *saptabhangi* is the earliest anticipation of this.

In the recent literature on relativity, space and time are not considered to be separate from each other but are linked up in a sort of inseparable relation so that one could not conceive of one without conceiving the other. In consequence, instead of talking of space and time, as has hitherto been customary, it is now a habit to talk of space-time as a single object, or as facets of the same object. One of the popular expositions of relativity has been given by Viscount Haldane wlich is, in part, as follows:

> The idea that there is an absolute framework of time and a quite independent absolute framework of space is not easy to avoid. For, we have been schooled to it . . . But if both space and time are stripped of what is unessential, and presented in their bare nakedness, they look different. If there were no succession in time, and everything appeared as at one instant, a little reflection shows that we could not apprehend the positions of points in space. Their reality depends for us on their separation,

which itself depends on transition, and this on succession in time. On the other hand, if, in the absence of all separation in space, there were only one spatial point in which existence centred for us as time elapsed, it is equally clear that intervals of time would have no meaning. Duration would be immesaurable, for, it is by spatialising, as on the dial of a watch, that we measure it. Space and time are really abstractions from a reality which includes both in mutual implication.

—Viscount Haldane, *The Reign of Relativity*, p. 46

There are two important consequences of modern relativity, one on the theory of matter, and the other on the nature of knowing. As to the first, as the old concepts of absolute space and absolute time are replaced by a combined space-time, the conception of matter has undergone a modification from that which 'is' to that which 'happens', from an atom to an event, or, as Whitehead has put it, a bit of matter "is as much an instant of time as it is a point of space." The Jainas introduced no such modification in their idea of matter. As to the second, philosophers have now recognised two characteristics of knowing, viz., its dependence upon, and variation with, points of view, or perspective, and its claim to disclose the essence of things. But there is an apparent contradiction between the two. For, when knowing discloses the essence of things, why should it vary according to perspective, and anything which varies according to perspective can have no essence which it may call its own. The western philosophers who have recognised relativity are yet to recognise their shortcoming in this respect. The Jaina doctrine of *sapta-bhangi* already discussed is not only the earliest anticipation of relativity, but also a wonderful texture of relativity with the essence of things. In this there is no contradiction anywhere.

As the scientific doctrine of relativity has emerged in the arena of mathematics and physics, the theologists of the Christian world have felt no alarm about their conception of an absolute God and have not raised any hue and cry against it as they did against Darwin's doctrine of creative evolution. But the Jaina *anekantavada* goes straight into the very heart of religion and the reaction of the Hindu absolutists against it has been bitter. The earliest reaction came from the *advaita* philosophers like Sankar and Ramanuja who pointed at the impossibility of contradictory attributes co-existing in the same thing. Thus Ramanuja wrote,

> Contradictory attributes such as existence and non-existence cannot at the same time belong to one thing any more than light and darkness.

This is a total distortion of the Jaina stand. If a pot is made of gold, surely it is not made of silver, copper or brass, and the Jainas never say that it is simultaneously made of all these. If still *anekantavada* was misunderstood and misinterpreted by both Sankara and Ramanuja, it was not because they were small men, but because their perspective was tied to an emotionalism in which they found the doctrine of *anekanta* to be wholly inconsistent. But the position has not improved even now. Two examples will be of use.

To M. Hiriyanna (his *Outlines of Indian Philosophy* and *Popular Essays in Indian Philosophy*), *anakantavada* has appeared as an acme of 'philosophic fastidiousness'; it is a 'conception of reality (which is) extremely indeterminate in its nature', and is the outcome of an 'extreme caution and signifies an anxiety to avoid all dogmas in defining the nature of reality'. Hiriyanna makes no secret to denounce the Jaina doctrine as a half-hearted thing which 'leaves us in the end with little more than one-sided solutions. He attributes this half-heartedness to two reasons, viz., first, it is the outcome not of a prejudice against absolutism but of a 'desire to keep close to common belief,' and second, Hiriyanna says, the Jainas are not bothered about the ultimate solution of the metaphysical problem. As to the first, two objections suggest themselves at once, viz., first, it is difficult to understand wherefrom Hiriyanna derived the notion that Jainism has no prejudice against absolutism when the fact is just the reverse, and, second, if Jainism had really cared to keep close to common beliefs, it would not have dared to repudiate the very notion of God which is the commonest of all common beliefs. And as to the second, Hiriyanna is very unfair to Jainism. In being so, he has not only relegated a very important item in Jaina religious thought to a mere secondary position, he has even discounted the value of Jainism in the solution of the metaphysical problem.

To S. Radhakrishnan, the notion of the 'relative' cannot stand in the absence of an absolute, and since the Jainas are stuck up in their own *anekantavada*, they are 'untrue to their own logic.' This is a very serious charge. To him,

> the distinction between subject and object is not a relation between two independent entities but a distinction made by knowledge itself within its own field ... Before any question of knowledge arises, this one self must be presupposed as the ultimate and final fact within which follow all distinctions of subject and object.

Clearly, the entire reasoning is based on the assumption of 'one self' to which both subject and object, individual mind and independent reality, belong. But where, as in Jainism, this one self transcending all subjects and objects is not accepted, where distinction does not presuppose 'unity', but is valid throughout, where a vast multiplicity of *jivas* and *ajivas* is no mere intellectual tool, but a major premise, the charge of Jainism being untrue to its own logic does not stand.

Radhakrishnan's crusade does not stop at this. He seeks to assess the Jaina view, and ultimately assigns it a place at the kindergarten stage of the developed monistic view. In his words,

> The fact that we are conscious of our relativity means that we have to reach out to a fuller conception ... With continuous advance towards fuller and fuller truth, the object itself loses its apparently given character. When we reach absolute knowledge, the distinction between subject and object is overcome. Only in the light of such an absolute standard could we correct the abstractions of the lower. Then we shall see that the several relatives are only stages in a continuous process which has the realisation of the soul's freedom for its determining end. The recognition of every form of knowledge as relative, something bound to pass over into something else requires us to assume a larger reality, an absolute, into which all tle relatives fall ... The Jainas cannot logically support a theory of pluralism.

—S. Radhakrishnan, *Indian Philosophy*, Vol. I, Chapter 6

This is a very severe attack on the Jaina *anekantavada* which tantamounts to a complete misrepresentation of the doctrine. The assumption of a 'larger reality' dominates his whole outlook and everything else is sought to fit in with it. But the Jainas do not recognise any such larger reality which the monists do, and hence the Jainas are in no way illogical to their own pluralism.

A more appreciative view is expressed by S. N. Dasgupta when he writes,

> The solution of Jainism is . . . a reconciliation of the two extremes of Vedantism and Buddhism.
>
> —S. N. Dasgupta, *History of Indian Philosophy*, Vol. I

If this real notion of the empirical reality appears more complicated than the abstract notion of a transcendental reality, the fault does not lie in the notion, but in the essence of reality. As C. W. Miller says,

> It reminds one of a great mountain which represents a particular contour when approached from one direction but an entirely different aspect from another. Only as we live in the many valleys that nestle into its flanks and as we climb through its ravines and its ridges can we truly say that we know the mountain.
>
> —C. W. Miller, *A Scientist's Approach to Religion*

The main reason why the Indian systems have failed to appreciate the scientific accuracy of *anekantavada* is that while the Jainas have viewed reality as it is, others, being baffled by its variety and multiplicity have rejected it outright and erected in its place an imaginary structure called the transcendental reality. As the Upanisad says, 'One I become many' (*ekohaham vahusyam*). If empirical reality is conceived to emanate from a transcendental reality, it is also conceived to terminate in the latter, to re-emanate from it again. In this view, the only thing permanent is the transcendental reality; all else is to be understood in terms of it. This type of view is basically different from the Jaina view of reality which is all a timeless plurality. In breaking away from the absolutist myth, the Jainas have not been a victim of any illogicity; rather, their whole logic is securely founded in their very notions of *jiva* and *ajiva* both of which are innumerable and beyond count. They have nither emanated from an absolute, like a tree from a seed, nor do they ever merge back into any absolute. But even here the monistic writers have tried to put a distorted interpretation of the Jaina view by suggesting that since the entire variety of the physical universe is one kind of substance called *pudgalas*, and since all the *jivas* are a second kind, and since the two are in actual relation with each other, there must be a superior third party to establish this relation. To quote Hiriyanna again,

> The necessary implication of Jaina thought in this respect is, therefore, a single spiritual substance encountering a single material substance. And since these substances are interdependent, the dualism must in its turn and finally be resolved in a monism.

The word 'interdependent' in the above quotation is misconceived, because the contact between *jiva* and *ajiva* does not lead to an interdependence arranged through the agency of a third party, nor is the contact inseparable. The Jaina doctrines of relativity and plurality thus stand on an invincible foundation. It is an utter misrepresentation of the Jaina logic and a total misrepresentation of the Jaina view to suggest that since all *ajivas* are identical, and since they are interdependent with the *jivas*, the two, the *jivas* and the *ajivas*, could just be bundled together and hugged into an imaginary absolute.

BIBLIOGRAPHY

PRAKRIT

Acharanga (first srutaskandha)
Sutrakritanga (Vira-tthui-prakarana)
Sthananga (sta. 10)
Vyakhya Prajnapti (sataka 15)
Uvasaga Dasao
Antagada Dasao
Aupapatika
Bhagavati
Avasyak Niryukti and Churni
Kalpa Sutra
Mahavira Charitra by Nemichandra Suri
Mahavira Charitra by Gunachandra Sur
Chaupana-mahapurisa-chariyam by Silanka Dhavala

SANSKRIT

Uttara-purana by Gunasena
Tri-sasti-salaka-purusa-charitram by Hemachandra
Vardhaman Purana by Asaga
Vardhamana Kavya by Padmanandi
Vardhamana Charitra by Sakala Kirti
Mahavira Purana by Asadhara

APAVRAMSA

Mahapurana by Puspadanta
Vaddhamana Chariu by Jayamitra
Vaddhamana Kaha by Narasena
Vaddhamana Kavya by Harischandra
Vaddhamana Charium by Vibudha Sridhara

ENGLISH

Lord Mahavira by Harisatya Bhattacharya
Lord Mahavira, a study in historical perspective, by Bool Chand
Bhagavan Mahavira by Chauthmal (muni)
Tirthankara Mahavira by K. P. Jain

205

Lord Mahavira and some other teachers of his time by K. P. Jain
Mahavira: his life and teachings by B. C. Law
Mahavira: his life and teachings by Raghavachari, S
Sramana Bhagavan Mahavira (8 volumes) by Ratna-prabhavijaya
                                      (muni)
Lord Mahavira: his life and doctrines by P. C. Samsookha